My Mother Would Hate This Book

Marcia Seligson

Praise for *My Mother Would Hate This Book*

"Marcia Seligson is one of the funniest, most original, and irreverent people I know, and her book carries all those qualities. She can make anything funny, from a Peloton bike to a 40-hour brisket cookery. And she can be touching, deep, and bracingly honest. My advice to readers is make sure you have unbroken time ahead when you pick up this book. Each time I did, intending to read for ten minutes, an hour went by before I looked up. And I'd laughed out loud at least twice."

—Sara Davidson
*Writer of the NY Times bestseller **Loose Change**
Head writer for **Dr. Quinn, Medicine Woman***

"Marcia Seligson's unique wit enlivens every anecdote, her characters are vivid and true, her tone both self-mocking and endearing, and her hard-won smarts zing off the page and into your heart. This book is an effervescent cocktail of champagne with a shpritz of seltzer for good measure."

—Letty Cottin Pogrebin
*A founding editor of Ms. Magazine and author of
SHANDA: A Memoir of Shame and Secrecy*

"How thrilling to discover a unique literary voice with an equally unique story to tell. In these finely crafted essays, author Marcia Seligson regales us with hilarious and touching postcards of her amazing life—sharing a true Rocky Mountain high with John Denver, seeking shamans in Peru, chasing Mother Teresa around India—with a wit and insight increasingly rare these days. What an incredibly eventful road she's traveled and how joyously she takes us along for the ride!"

—Duane Poole
Screenwriter/playwright/producer

"A charming and chatty memoir in which she incidentally takes drugs, defies the establishment, walks with lions in Africa, tames naughty superstars and has sex with at least one of them. This is a life worth reading about!"

—Bruce Vilanch
Emmy-winning writer and Hollywood Square

"Marcia Seligson has lived a jumbo-sized and out loud life! Her latest, *My Mother Would Hate This Book*, is filled with fabulous adventures. I'm delighted to have played a small part in one of them. Marcia heeded the sage advice of Auntie Mame, 'Life is a banquet.' Marcia has clearly savored every bite!"

—Melissa Manchester
Grammy Award winning singer/songwriter

"Marcia Seligson's book is like her life: a constantly surprising delight! Smart, funny, moving, rambunctious, sexy, unruled by bourgeois manners, daring and undaunted—that's Marcia, and that's her brazen and bountiful book! Don't be mean to yourself—read It!"

—Arthur Allan Seidelman
Emmy-winning director of theater, television, and film

"Marcia Seligson tells it exactly like it is, with heartfelt humor and love. She writes what all of us are thinking, but often afraid to say out loud—and she writes it with joy and gusto that implore us to dive into her life's journey with her. Once I got in, I couldn't put this collection of essays on a life lived large, down. She's a brilliant raconteur and full of fun."

—Sheilah Rae
Writer/songwriter/theater Junkie

"Marcia Seligson, you are writing about MY LIFE! Between guffaws at the cleverness on every page, I shake my head in rueful recognition that you are such a fine observer of the hilarious vagaries of daily life. I am going to carry this book in my pocket wherever I go, so I can be reminded to laugh at all life has to offer. A wonderful, insightful read!"

—*Amanda McBroom*

Actress/Golden Globe-winning songwriter of the Bette Midler classic **The Rose**

"The consummate hostess, Marcia Seligson opens her doors, metaphorically, to a life well lived. This breezy book of memories is a delightful ride that you will find yourself devouring in one sitting!!!!!!!!!!"

—*Andrea Marcovicci*

Actress/singer

"When I think Producer…I think Marcia Seligson. Marcia has always been the real deal. A leader in the Los Angeles theater community and beyond. Having the opportunity to look behind the scenes of her incredible adventures is a delicious, not-to-be-missed treat. Read this book. Then read it again! You won't be sorry."

—*Brian Kite*

Director, Professor and Interim Dean of the UCLA School of Theater, Film and Television

"Marcia Seligson spills her guts, spills the tea, tells it all, says the quiet part out loud with charm, wit and humor in this delightful tour of her eclectic, accomplished and charmed life. My mother would have loved this book. I certainly do."

—*David Zippel*

Tony Award-winning lyricist/director/producer

"An easy breezy hoot of a hang-out with a fun-loving second-wave feminist. Her close encounters with Steven Spielberg and Mother Teresa as a writer-for-hire, her recurring themes of the Peloton, brisket and her Aunt Fritzi, her escapades producing big musicals with midget-minded celebrities kept her book hanging in my hands for a seamless read. Maybe her mother wouldn't like it, but I sure did, and I think you will, too."

—Melanie Chartoff
*Actor, author, **Odd Woman Out:***
Exposure in Essays and Stories

"Pure joy. *My Mother Would Hate This Book* is a blissful romp through Marcia Seligson's extraordinary life. Picking it up is like getting together with a dear old friend—which makes it hard to put down."

—Sam Daley-Harris
Founder, RESULTS and Civic Courage
*Author, **Reclaiming Our Democracy***

"Marcia is an accomplished pianist, journalist, theatrical producer who's interviewed Mother Teresa, sung with John Denver and worked with Steven Spielberg. Her storytelling is tight, fast, and fun, covering family relationships, theatre, consciousness-raising and myriad travel adventures. Her mother might hate this book, but you will love her honesty, transparency, energy and spirit."

—Adryan Russ
Theater, film, TV and recording lyricist/composer

My Mother Would Hate This Book

Marcia Seligson

AMARNA
BOOKS & MEDIA
www.amarnabooksandmedia.com

ISBN: 979-8-9859674-0-1

Book design by Thomas Edward West of Amarna Books & Media.

Photography credits: front cover, Tom Drucker; back cover: Anglebert Pantaleo

First print edition 2022

AMARNA BOOKS & MEDIA
Maplewood, New Jersey
www.amarnabooksandmedia.com

Dedication

To Tom. For everything in life.

Acknowledgments

I couldn't and wouldn't have written this book without the applause, laughter and huzzahs from my writing workshop. Thanks beyond thanks to Claudette, Sheena, Ellen, Stef and Kay. No appropriate cheers exist for Duane and his endless encouragement. To all my friends and family who remembered that I once wrote books for a living. To Bryant Chase for his social media brilliance and Maxine Carter for her daily laughter-filled commitment. Bless you to Sheilah Rae for introducing me to Thomas Edward West at Amarna Books and Media and bows and scrapes to Tom West himself.

Contents

Foreword

You know how there are times when you want nothing more than to settle down with a good friend, have a long talk about life knowing you will come away eager for more? Marcia Seligson is that friend you will find in this collection of snapshots of her well-lived life. There are sections tasty as a memorable meal or colorful as an album of travel photos to places you have longed to visit. Also, you will engage in a little gossip, which is often the salt and pepper of stories.

I had the good fortune of tagging along with Marcia as she developed these pieces in workshop. I found myself waiting weekly to be transported to Africa, eavesdropping on a conversation with John Denver, waiting for a UFO in the desert with Steven Spielberg, or sitting in on her in-person meeting with Mother Teresa. Exotic as these pieces were, it was the domestic with which I identified. Her marriage to Tom, her beloved husband of forty years, is the canvas upon which all these scenes are framed. If there were such a thing as a perfect marriage, this would qualify as a model. He is Abelard to her Eloisa.

Marcia's stoic acceptance of Tom's fanciful obsession with cookware that promises to change their lives is equaled only by the question of where in their apartment to store the shiny, but seldom-used, appliance. Noteworthy too, was the short-lived experience with the complex Peloton system of fitness designed to bring a couple closer together. It did. They both agreed it was a disaster.

As if all this wasn't theatrical enough Marcia, later in life bored with the isolated life of writing; she became drawn to her early love of musical theatre. She created and produced REPRISE, BROADWAY'S BEST, a series of classic musicals for Los Angeles audiences ranging from *Finian's Rainbow* to *Hair* to *Sweeney Todd*.

This is a romp of a read. You will fall in love with Marcia. It left me wanting to have married a "Tom". And oh yes, there is a dog: Roxie.

—Claudette Sutherland
Writer/actor/teacher

Tom

Early Days With Tom

I had just come back from India searching for Mother Teresa (more about that elusive saint later), and I went to a meeting where I met Tom, my husband of forty years. I went because I wanted to confront Billy, the boyfriend I'd had before I left the country, for whom I'd brought back an expensive, embroidered silk shirt. I gave it to him at the airport when he picked me up, and after he opened it and exclaimed its beauty, he told me he'd met somebody else while I was gone. I called him the next day, furious, and demanded the shirt back. He was reluctant but I was adamant, so he promised he'd bring it to this gathering the following Monday.

The event was a meeting of a bunch of shrinks, New Age educators, and folks interested in creating a weekend conference at UCLA. The group met every Monday night at somebody's home in Santa Monica, working to shape the conference. Tom was a psychologist who had just moved back to LA, his hometown, after spending several years working for the Xerox Company in Connecticut. His goal was to make business and social connections. I had never been to this jolly and impressive gathering before. I only went to reclaim the blue shirt.

A friend named—no kidding—Victor Herbert was a smart, retired fifty-year-old who loved to hang out with other smart New Age people, and went to these get-togethers every week. I told him the sad tale of my lost affair and he said, "Of course come with me on Monday, we'll handle the whole thing with Billy and get the damn shirt back."

Several days later I stood inside the front hall of the Segals' welcoming home, talking to several people I knew. When a handsome man with wavy black hair walked in, Victor brought him over to introduce me and said the basic life-changing words: "Marcia Seligson, this is Tom Drucker." Something went off inside me and I said (to myself of course), "I'm going to marry him." I knew nothing at all about him—was he... Single? Attached? Gay? Poor? I'd never had this thought before, even during the one brief time I was engaged seventeen years earlier. But the bizarre thing was that I felt I'd known Tom forever, that we were connected before we'd had a single conversation. When we compared notes a few months later, he confessed he had had none of these feelings. He just thought I was cute and sexy.

I never did get the shirt back from Billy.

Tom and I bonded very quickly, did all the usual dinner/movies/sex things, discovered we had been on the same sailing of the ship, the Queen Elizabeth, to England many years before, me off to visit family in London, him off to his junior year abroad at the University of Vienna. Our synchronistic lives mounted up: EST, psychedelics, mutual friends, roller skating, New Age philosophy, passion for beef ribs.

One morning we traveled to Topanga Canyon to visit Sara, an opera singer who supported herself by giving colonics. We had connected with her at the aforementioned meeting, she gave me her card which I unearthed one day for fun, and off we went. She set us up in her "treatment room", which had fabrics covering every wall, two massage tables next to one another, a cloth barrier between them. While she gave us the colonics, she sang operatic arias, not very well at that, but at least they distracted me from this weird, impossible scene. Tom seemed totally comfortable.

By then, he was spending most of his time at my home in the Hollywood Hills, and we spent our weekends at his tiny apartment on the Venice boardwalk roller skating, barbecuing steaks, and strolling the beach. He met all my friends and they approved. I met his family and thought they were peculiar. I don't know to this day if they approved of me.

One night our friend David picked us up at my house. We were having dinner with a few pals at Roy's Chinese restaurant on the Sunset Strip. In the car, David said: "Ok, it's time you got engaged." We'd been together about four months. "If you do, I'll buy dinner," he continued, "if you don't, you buy dinner."

Tom and I searched each other's faces and quickly agreed. Our potential engagement and future wedding became THE topic of conversation at Roy's hip bistro until, finally, Tom said, "OK, how about the wedding a year from now?" I grimaced, implying that was too far away. "OK," he backed off, "how about six months?" "That's too soon," I reacted. "I can't plan a wedding in only six months." It looked for a moment as if this marriage would not be consummated based on our differing timetables. We compromised at a date eight months in the future and Roy, the owner, got very excited and brought us champagne and dessert to share at our table.

When we got home we called Donna, our astrologer friend, and told her the date we'd chosen. She cautioned that on that date Mercury was in retrograde, which I didn't understand—I still don't—but I know bad things happen and you don't want to make ANY serious commitments during Mercury's dark period.

So, the next morning we selected February 28, checked it out with Donna the astrologer, who said the planets approved, and that was the beginning of our forty years of marriage.

Letter to Tom

Dear Tom,

   You know that I love you with all my heart. And I'm begging you to clean up your office. I'm still stunned, even after forty years together, what a huge mess you create. How can you live with it, work and be creative and successful and somehow find a paper that's buried in a graveyard of other papers somewhere on your substantial desk space? The junk—at least I think it's junk—also inhabits the couch, the other chairs, the other desk, and the floor. It scares me. But you don't seem to notice or care. I can't even find a paper clip in your entire universe, even though I know it's there somewhere. Somewhere.

We're very different in many ways, my darling husband, this being a substantial one. It's not that I'm compulsively neat or organized; it's obvious I'm not. My desk is crowded with stuff, including random papers, two dishes of various-sized post-its, and a bottle of Pepto Bismol. But it's not deranged like yours, and sometimes I do find the urge to do a serious straightening up of my space and feel a grand surge of relief when my desk is back to a normal state of repair.

But you, dear heart: when you feel too embarrassed to go on with your office as it is, or if we're having any friends come over, you gather all the mess in piles on the floor in the corners and cover them with the lovely area rugs we've brought back from all over the world, which should, of course, be sitting there in their rightful rug places. But they are, you believe, disguising the junk as they hover over the obvious lumps underneath. Dearest one, they are hiding nothing at all.

One of the lumps includes the giant Instant Pot you insisted on buying because you've gotten involved in cooking during the Covid years, for the first time in our lives together. And part of your joy of cooking is all the redundant utensils you have bought, like three whisks and a dozen measuring cups to complement the dozen we already own. I took a firm stand: I would not get involved with the Instant Pot and all its incorporated gadgets, like the air fryer and the pressure cooker. This was your project; I insisted there was no room in the pantry closet, so you said you'd keep it in your office—a strange location, you admitted, for a vast kitchen toy. And there it lives, covered over, but not hidden, by the small brightly colorful rug we brought back from India. You've only used the Instant Pot once in the three months we've had it because the top broke and they haven't sent a new one yet.

My sweetheart, you are so much more generous than I. Some might call it extravagant. I remember when we were redoing our bathroom before we moved into our current home, thirty years ago. You stopped at a giant appliance store and picked up a brochure for a bathtub that you fell in love with. It cost about $6,000. Even our decorator was appalled. I was doubly stunned because, in addition to the outrageous cost, I'd never seen you take a bath—you were and are a shower guy. We didn't buy it.

Your generosity moves me, how much you tip people, how much you donate to the various charities we support, how much you will pay for steaks at our local supermarket. I do not have this gene. But sometimes it panics me, I worry about our running out of money, and you must soothe me with your calmness and optimistic assurance that we're okay, we will always be okay. It works. I believe you; I know you wouldn't buy a $40 steak at Gelson's if it meant we would have to sell our home.

My darling: how can you believe *Saturday Night Live* is funny? I think that it's stupid and I watch it with you just as part of the Great Compromise that befits a successful marriage, along with my never putting my beloved arugula in our salad because you hate any sort of what you call bitter lettuce. With *SNL*, I have noticed that I never laugh, even once during an episode, and I keep hoping you'll say something like, "Boy, this sure isn't funny, let's watch a rerun of *Law & Order* instead." But you never do, so I swallow my churlishness. Sometimes I'll just read my email on my phone while the dumb show is playing, hoping you'll notice and switch channels, but it doesn't happen. OK, a small thing, I admit.

In the confined time of Covid, when we spent almost every evening watching TV instead of dining with friends or going to the movies, theatre, or a concert, compromise is central to our love for each other. When all I want is to curl up with a historical French romantic drama on Netflix and you want to watch an animated science fiction thing, we do neither and one of us just says, "I'll watch that some other time when you're not around." And we end up binging on one of our precious British murder mystery series, both of us content.

Tom my dearest, I treasure how you support my writing and producing efforts, how you send my pieces to all your business colleagues, how you always tell me how proud you are of me and what I do. You are the kindest person I know, and the least judgmental of others. I learn from you every day how to be more kind myself, just by watching you and listening to you on the phone with other people.

I adore how you behave with our blessed pup Roxie, how much you clearly worship her. And I can't wait for you to cook chicken wings in our new air fryer, which is waiting patiently under the green and red Peruvian rug in your office.

All my love,

Marcia

Oh, Food Food Food

F ood consumes—please forgive the awful pun—
so much of my time. Not necessarily eating but
thinking about what we should have for tonight's
and tomorrow night's dinners, as well as reflecting
on the sensational pasta Bolognese we ate last night,
delivered from our favorite local Italian restaurant.
The leftovers made a happy lunch. I remembered
it all day.

I was recently dumbstruck and rather horrified to
notice how much of my normal waking day is spent
focusing on food: not eating as I said, but cogitating,
talking, planning, shopping, reading recipes online,
watching the Food Network instead of depressing
news about Republicans on CNN. A minor amount
of actual cooking takes place.

Here's an example of my food involvement: I was having a Pilates session, always a deep and forceful experience. Suddenly my very thin, muscular instructor asked me about restaurants in West LA, where she lives. I went through most of the menu of my favorite Taiwanese spot, Little Fatty. This conversation took place during a particularly strenuous series of stretches on the Pilates Reformer machine. I didn't mind, it carried my thoughts away from my pain. Then she told me, unasked, in detail, about the Mexican cafe in her neighborhood, and all its unique dishes. I pretended to be interested because she was so excited to be talking about food.

After Pilates I drove crosstown to meet four girlfriends who have lunch together once a month. That day we had many discussions about, guess what? FOOD. We shared French fries, summoned the waitress several times for extra aglio e olio dressing, took bites of each other's salads, and heard a long detailed story about one of the friend's dreadful recent experiences at a local popular restaurant. She then read us her entry on Yelp, detailing every moment of the dinner from hell, followed by the restaurant's refutation, in which they called her a liar. All of us were deeply involved with her tale of food woe.

After lunch, I stopped by the nearby supermarket for their fresh fish and deli egg salad and chicken salad. Somehow, I managed to spend $68 on not very much. I came home and made a sandwich for

Tom. It was now about 3:30 and I had spent most of the day focused in some way on food. I then figured out dinner and marinated the fish, cutting up veggies for roasting to accompany it.

Later that same afternoon I went walking with my friend Susan and our dogs. Certain topics of conversation always come up: There's politics, some gossip, and any new discoveries we've made on television or books. But then there's the inevitable "what are you having for dinner tonight?" I'm usually jealous because her menus are more creative and fancier than mine. Mine often involve a delivery from the Fresh Brothers pizza palace or a turkey meatloaf from Trader Joe's.

When I started to think about how much of my attention is given to food, I envisioned a ladder sliding down from my home directly into my mother's early kitchen. She was a Russian immigrant of a fairly poor Jewish background. I imagine that although food wasn't plentiful in her family or community, it was still critical, and the origin of some of my obsessiveness as well as my lifelong favorite dishes. Pot roasts, thick soups, potato anything, roasted chickens with crispy skins, sweet apple cake. There were no frozen foods then to defrost nightly, no Chinese delivery. Everything was fresh, some dishes started their cooking journeys right after breakfast and continued for many hours. I'm sure the smells permeated her home all day.

Food made these people from poor countries,

oppressed by their cultures, feel somewhat safe, protected. If my family can eat a hearty hot chicken soup with matzo balls for dinner, how much danger can I be in? This mentality has passed down for hundreds of years in my family's world along with the pot roast recipe.

This connection of food with safety continues. My friend Helene, whose parents were in several concentration camps during the Holocaust, always has food in her purse, a protein bar or something else light and small. She told me: "I never go anywhere without food on me. I almost never eat anything, or very much, but what if something happens? I have to know food is there." In her home, her giant freezer is overflowing, even though her husband cooks fresh and substantial meals every night.

Everybody took up cooking while isolated during the pandemic: no restaurants open for a long time, fears of delivery people not wearing masks or not being vaccinated, worries about strange people touching the food. We didn't even go to markets, just ordered stuff delivered from the local grocery store. Or went there at 6 a.m. when they allowed a handful of humans to come in, provided we were masked and socially distanced. I loathe getting up at 6:00 in the morning but it seemed the appropriate thing to do.

During that year, 2020, Tom embraced cooking. He had never toasted an English muffin in our thirty-eight years together, but he found his gizmo The

Instant Pot online and bought it immediately. As I've written earlier, it's a combo air fryer, pressure cooker, sous vide cooker (don't ask), slow cooker and roaster. In my view it's absurdly complicated and he's had to return it twice because of mechanical flaws, he's only used it once, but it does make heavenly chicken wings. He hasn't tried anything else.

One of my life's pleasures is eating in bed. Friends think it's icky and probably tomato sauce gets all over the sheets but it's not that way. We have the kind of bed whose head and foot move up and down. So I can sit up tall, stretch out my legs, move the sheet and quilt out of the way so it doesn't get hit by the sauce, put the food dishes on my lap, and neatly pose myself as if I were in a chair.

Next, we turn on the TV and we're in food escape heaven. We've even trained our dog Roxie to stay sitting on the carpet, away from the food, while we're eating. After dinner, we don't have to think or talk about food until the next morning when we discuss what we're going to have for dinner.

The Worst Meal in Forty Years

O n the first night of Hanukah Tom and I had the worst meal we had eaten in the forty years of our marriage. Well, since we threw most of it down the garbage disposal, I'm exaggerating to call it the worst "meal".

I'm a good cook, of the Russian Jewish variety, with lots of Italian and a bit of Chinese wok thrown in. I love to make hearty, meaty dishes that must cook for a few hours, so that if I forget the exact minute to extract them from the pot or oven, it doesn't make any difference. I don't bake, poach, make desserts, prepare anything delicate, or cook any fish but pan-broiled. I don't bother with recipes that have ingredients I can't pronounce or find at Gelson's or Trader Joe's. I make the best brisket on the planet.

Tom studied chemistry, doesn't normally cook much, and is a bit OCD—obsessive-compulsive disordered. Not long ago, he bought this gizmo, a "sous vide" cooker, which featured a very large plastic container and several other incomprehensible pieces. He started cooking steaks and lamb chops in it, the only dishes he ever prepared. "I'm experimenting", he announced happily as he shoved the cooker into the pantry closet, taking up much of the limited space. I swore: "OK, it's your game, do what you will, but I'm not using it or cleaning it." And I never have.

Sous vide, in French, means "under vacuum", which says that the food is sealed in a plastic bag to cook with all the air removed. The bag is submerged in water that is raised electrically to a low temperature and cooked much longer than conventional time. The use of the bag, the water bath, the minimal temperature, and the extended cooking time results, God willing, in superior taste, texture, and aroma. I can only say it looks very weird to see a thick steak in the container surrounded by gurgling water but, in fact, I can swear that it produces the best steaks I've ever tasted. No kidding...

Tom is gleeful in explaining to me the details: "The fan at the bottom circulates the water, keeping it hot. I suck the air out with a straw. A rare steak cooks for an hour." He is beyond eager and he begins reading recipes and figuring out his upcoming adventure. Then he discovers the forty-hour brisket. "Forty hours?" I shriek. "That can't be. My divine brisket cooks for three hours and it's perfect, juicy, flavorful, and tender." He insists the brisket that's submerged for a day and a half, oh yes, and then continues cooking in the oven for another three hours, has gotten the best reviews on a website that caters to dozens of brisket-obsessed chefs.

I warn him that when he puts it in the sous vide, I will jump on a plane to Hong Kong and arrive back home just in time for dinner. Or I will use a sleeping bag on the kitchen floor for two nights, in case something scary happens with the electricity and the whole machine explodes. He thinks I'm wacko, of course. I take neither path. Periodically, I check in on the brisket but I can't see anything happening, and I just hear a soft hum from the fan.

We tell various friends what Tom is doing. Our funny friend Carole says: "Anybody who embraces this idea needs help. What could possibly happen at forty hours that you wouldn't get at three hours?" Steve says: "Tom's got more time on his hands than he should."

He finally succeeds at the beginning of Hanukah, and the optimum holiday dinner of brisket emerges from the long bath. It looks to me like a dead chunk of animal that we've seen on the plains of Tanzania. But I'm hopeful, and Tom is worked up. Tragically, he's having trouble getting the big knife to pierce into it. Finally, he succeeds in cutting a small piece off the side and we bite. It's tough, tasteless, and reeking with salt. And it still must cook for another three hours in the oven.

"What is going on?" I wail. "I can't imagine," he wails back. "I followed the prize recipe exactly." We both make an instant decision to laugh through this instead of getting upset. It's only meat, although more money than I like to think about. We call our friend Eddie, a master chef, desperate. He says: "Slice it very thin, make a gravy of the juice, red wine, and beef broth and stick it in the oven for an hour."

We still have hope. To no avail. The brisket that emerges from the oven is hopeless. Hopeless. After it cools, we put it down the garbage disposal and settle in for our Hanukah supper of Häagen-Dazs peanut butter ice cream. There are two cuts for brisket—one is perfect, the other should never have left the cow. Tom admitted, "I think I chose the wrong one."

We realize this has been a special event: even with all our travels through the third world, eating tarantulas in Thailand and sheep innards in Africa, we've never had anything that tasted so vile, we agreed, howling.

The next day Tom announces that he is going to try it again, using a different recipe that calls for twenty-five hours of cooking instead of forty. "It's an experiment", he insisted. "This time I'll get it right." I've said nothing.

Two Jews and A Peloton

It seemed like such a good idea at the time. Our gym has been closed for almost two years; walking has been okay but not serious exercise. And Tom and I used to be committed bike riders, witness fourteen yearly trips to Europe, Canada, and Nova Scotia, including pedaling through the Swiss Alps. I kept seeing Peloton ads with buff young people in terrific exercise outfits hauling ass in front of a screen while teachers prodded and nudged them.

Our first of several mistakes: we didn't go to a Peloton store to try it out; we just bought it on the phone. We also had to buy special shoes to clamp onto the pedals. I knew it was going to be high-tech;

I'm a total tech dork and was nervous well before it arrived. Everybody we talked to loves the Peloton, relishes the screen attachments—yoga sessions, spinning classes, online biking trips through New Zealand and other extravagant spots. But I noticed that everybody we spoke to is a few decades younger than we are.

When the sweet man delivered it and set it up in the den six weeks after we bought it—oh yes, they were back-ordered, sales were booming—Tom was delighted, I was wary.

We had to hook the special cleated shoes which cost $150 a pair onto the pedals each time we got on the bike, which seemed an impossible feat. The patient delivery fellow helped by jerking my right leg around to secure my pedal connection and my funky right knee twisted in pain. I asked him if we couldn't just wear regular sneakers and not go through that improbable torture. He was adamant and looked insulted. No, he insisted, the whole point was to be hooked onto this creature as if we were one being.

OK. I surrendered. I hated the Peloton already and I hadn't even pedaled yet. We had to use a mechanical lever to raise the seat (one height for Tom, another for me), to move the seat forward and back (we both had different requirements), and another to change the handlebar height. I didn't understand why we were putting ourselves through this Olympics. I found it all difficult to grasp and not the slightest bit fun. Way too complex for my aging brain and body. It was supposed to be a damn bicycle, for heaven's sake.

After the delivery guy left, obviously frustrated with me for my ineptness and nerves, I knew early on that I would never understand the Peloton beast, threatened Tom that I would never ride it. On the other hand, he was eager; he is labeled by friends Techno Tom, which is all you have to know about him and his relationship with the Peloton up to this point. He made me promise I would try it again, work to overcome my techno terror. I promised, although silently I knew the outcome.

We didn't ride the machine any longer that day. We each had a few glasses of cabernet instead. I whined to Tom, "I'm Jewish, I don't have a relationship with mechanical objects like this. I want to return it. I want a simple bike like I used to ride at the gym." He was annoyed I'd given up so quickly and pleaded with me to ride it again before making such an irreversible and grim judgment.

Then I called our dear friends Stef and Mark and begged, "Talk to Tom, tell him we're too old, tell him I'll have to have a knee replacement, remind him we're Jewish and klutzy." They laughed. Mark said, "I'll tell him he'll have to choose between you and the Peloton and see what he says." It was a week before our thirty-ninth anniversary.

The next day, after a restless sleep, I woke up dreading my next session with the hideous Peloton, but I had to go through with it. I felt guilty that Tom liked it so much and would be disappointed returning it. Tom had called the Peloton support number and told the fellow the major problem we were having was with clamping our shoes onto the pedals without torturing our backs and knees.

The helper was compassionate, according to Tom, and said we should buy something threateningly called "cages" which would hook permanently onto the pedals and make it simple to secure our shoes. They would FedEx the cages to us, so we'd be able to use them the next day. Reprieve! I wouldn't have to leap on the monster for another day. When they arrived, Techno Tom couldn't figure out how to put the cages on the pedals, and we had to get a handy neighbor to do it for us.

Tom also ordered a gel seat from Amazon to overcome the extreme discomfort of the original hard, tiny seat. It was scheduled to arrive in a few days. Another device to buy! Would the Peloton ever be complete? What would this endless device cost us?

We decided we always needed to be in the room with each other when we rode the bike in case some emergency arose. So, the next day after the new pedals were installed but before the new seat arrived, we went upstairs to the den. We each committed that we'd ride the Peloton for thirty minutes. I went first. Tom helped me get my shoes secured in the new pedals—not as simple as was promised, and I couldn't do it myself. I said, "Does this mean you'll always have to be with me when I get on the bike? That doesn't make sense." We didn't have an answer. We got the adjustments completed after many false tries and I touched the screen in order to bike through a Swiss town.

It was yet another disappointment. I remembered actually biking through the Swiss Alps years ago, the beauty of the mountain views, the villages, the water. The Peloton journey took me through a grim, gray city, not a tree or lake in sight. I rode for about ten minutes, feeling sore, bored, and uncomfortable the whole time—knees, shoulders, butt. I gave up.

Tom then got on the bike after my helping him secure the damn pedals onto his shoes, and he rode through New Zealand, a lovelier trip than my dreary Alpine jaunt. I sat on the couch, started reading the day's newspapers when he shrieked, "The seat did something to my ass!" He extricated himself from the bike. His ass was rubbed raw, the skin broken, and he was bleeding a bit. That was the final straw for both of us. And the final ride.

That afternoon he called Peloton to pick it up, exercising their thirty-day return policy. We packed up all the extras we had bought: the pedal cages, the cleat shoes, the gel seat. I was profoundly relieved, especially because Tom was no longer infatuated with the Peloton and eager to return it. Two days later, as they hauled it away, he shouted to me, "The Peloton has left the building."

Over the weekend, we found a fitness equipment store that got fine reviews on Yelp, we drove over there and bought the kind of stationary bike we should have had all along—simple, comfortable, a seat with a back, no need for special shoes or clamps, no dreary trips to Switzerland. The irony is that the company, Precor, is owned by Peloton. The perfect bike should arrive in a few days. I'm overjoyed. So is Techno Tom.

About Sleep

The problem with my sleep is that my brain doesn't rest, take a nap, or ever turn off. If I got paid for my brain's activity I would earn time-and-a-half in overtime for about sixteen hours a day. President Biden and Jeff Bezos might think this is a good thing. I do not. But I have no choice. Everything stirs up my brain, important as well as insignificant.

I can be lying in my lovely bed, happily drowsy, about to drift off to a perfect nap when suddenly I'll find myself fixated on voting rights in Arizona or whether our pooch Roxie was fed enough for breakfast. My brain is now tap dancing away, any idea of a nap having vanished. The thoughts can be serious—my brain considers the denial of voting rights quite grave—or somewhat trivial, like where is the package of face cream that Amazon was supposed to deliver today. Or absurd concerns, like do I have enough broccoli in the fridge to steam for dinner with the roast chicken. It doesn't seem to matter what level of importance the issue is, or if I may never worry about it again. Once I am obsessed with the topic, I'm obsessed and any thought of shoving it out of my head for a mere thirty or forty-five minutes of nap time is hopeless.

I do love sleeping—should you be thinking any indifference to sleep is the cause of the problem. Tom and I have a new Sleep Number king-sized bed, where the best part is that we are close bedmates but also independent. (Healthy for a long marriage, I say). We can each raise our head and feet portion without disturbing the other person. We can have our own level of mattress hardness or softness (he likes 100, the firmest, I vary from sixty to seventy-five. Sometimes if he wants to cocoon he takes it down to thirty and curls up; I would never think of doing that.)

My secret is that for him not to snore, his head section of the bed must be raised so that he's practically sitting up when he sleeps. If he forgets to raise it or doesn't do it high enough, and his snoring prevents me from dozing, I use the dual remote and lift him up until he stops the damn noise. Sometimes he wakes up, doesn't understand why he's sleeping sitting almost erect, and gets a bit annoyed in his confusion.

We have a new quilt, soft and mushy. I adore burrowing under it, will never again succumb to a boring blanket. And we each have three big pillows, one of which Roxie steals to sleep on most nights, which she places carefully next to my butt and cuddles right against me. Bless her, she doesn't move until I do in the morning.

Many mornings I am so comfy I truly HATE getting out of bed, getting vertical, getting dressed, and on with my day. Nothing hurts while I'm lying prostrate, my cranky back and chicken-bone right knee feel perfect. I keep promising myself that one day I'll stay in bed all day and do whatever I do from the supine position, periodically raising the bed to a sitting position and spreading out my work papers, my iPad, a container of yogurt, the tv remote, today's New York Times and my iPhone all around me. But I never do it. Maybe I'll write about guilt some other time.

Let me tell you about Tom and sleep, of which he is the master. Let's say we're meeting friends for dinner at 6:30 and he shuts down his home office at 5:45. So he has about twenty minutes to relax before we leave home. I'll be watching the news or reading the paper. He'll lie on the bed, turn on his alarm, declare "I'm going to close my eyes" and a split second later he's asleep. I really mean asleep, and I do mean instantaneously. He does it every time. I've queried him over and over about how he does that. I ask him, "where do you put your brain, your basket of thoughts, what worries might be left over from your workday?"

The only thing he has to say about it is "I learned to meditate while I was in college and I just go into that state when I want or need to sleep. Nothing overrides that unless I'm in physical pain." You can probably imagine that I am deeply jealous and when it happens and I'm next to him, I stare at him with envy and some resentment, wishing I could just figure out how he accomplishes this so I could do it too.

At bedtime, I fall asleep without much problem. Except for the night about every two weeks when I can't sleep at all, am not even a bit tired and after the cliché of endless tossing and turning, I go into the kitchen, turn on the tv to watch a rerun of *Friends*, and eat strawberry ice cream. It's all soothing and after one episode and half a pint, I can sleep. But a few weeks ago, I got absorbed in the movie *Erin Brockovich* which had the opposite effect. I watched an hour of the film, ate the whole pint of ice cream, and had trouble getting back to sleep until about 5 a.m. after pondering whatever happened to Erin and if the whole story was true or exaggerated.

Although I usually sleep well at night, I think the talent to nap at will is one of God's true blessings. How amazing to be able to turn everything off and drift into a serene slumber, wherever you are lying, or even sitting, for ten minutes or four hours, regardless of what activity and noise may be surrounding you. I have a hate-filled envy for those of you that have this gift. Me, I'm too worried about whether Donald Trump will run again, and I must stay alert.

I Hate Google

I have a favorite recurrent fantasy.

It is the 19th century; I am a rich lady living in a splendid villa in the countryside of France. I read loads of classic novels. They are actual books with black leather covers. When I want or need to communicate with somebody, I write a long and florid letter with a quill pen by candlelight, in my ornate handwriting. I then summon my horseman who leaps on his steed and rides off to deliver my notes directly to my people. He waits for their responses, then rides swiftly home to me with their letters.

To my mind, this is the perfect art of communication: personal, relaxed, speedy when need be, simple.

But life isn't like that anymore, is it? The computer, with all its complexities and, to me, its incomprehensibility, has altered our lives forever. Most people would say it's for the better (see how fast I'm typing this and correcting mistakes and looking up spelling); I say that for the most part it's jumbled my life in more ways than I value. When was the last time I sent somebody a letter or even a birthday card where I used a pen to write my message in longhand and had to look up their mailing address? When did I last use a stamp?

Oh, don't mistake me for a batty old lady in a rocking chair. I participate on Zoom meetings at least three times a week, and it's so much easier than driving twenty-seven miles to meet the friends in my women's group. We got used to this during the pandemic siege of course and many people I know, including Tom, are working happily from home, on Zoom with his clients and colleagues almost all day, wearing sweatpants, no ties, and bedroom slippers. I like Zoom. I wear mascara for it.

Like most people, I check the emails and text messages on my iPhone and Mac many times a day—too many times. That's the compulsive computer nut case in me. I always tell myself that I'll really stop looking every time I hear the "ping" signaling a new message and, if I'm not expecting anything important, I assure myself I'll only check messages twice a day. But who am I kidding?

I know most of the texts coming in will be from Nancy Pelosi and Joe Biden asking for money, but maybe there will be that one message inviting me to a private, glorious musical theatre event where there will only be forty-two guests and a handful of celebs, so I'd better be on top of this.

Years ago, I used to write *Playboy* Interviews, which were the length of entire books. Early on this was in the days of my Royal typewriter. I wrote pages and pages and spread them out all over the floor of my office to organize them into themes and topics. Then I cut and pasted, I mean literally cut with scissors and "pasted" with Scotch tape. If I had made a typo, I'd have to either retype the whole page or use whitener to erase and neatly retype the single word or phrase. How much easier is this process now, when cutting and pasting on my Mac is simple and quick? Make no mistake, I do indeed appreciate this aspect of computer life. Typing on my computer is my good pal.

But: I am basically a dork. I don't understand Google and all its permutations. I use the search function a lot, but I don't know anything about Google Maps, Gmail, their calendar, or Google drive and I don't care. I also don't understand all the initials that plague me constantly on my screen like PDF, DM, MP3 or MP4, URL. What am I supposed to do with them, except ignore them? And I have no patience for passwords. It seems to me every time I want to order a pair of shoes or doggie treats from Amazon, they require a different password from me, usually one I'm unfamiliar with. My mode of behavior is that I try once or twice, then give up and turn the project over to our assistant, who is in his early thirties and seems to me to be a genius at this stuff.

Now a question for readers: Do you really understand the ICloud? Do you care? Do you know anything about Linked In? I do not. Tom has tried to explain these to me many times, usually telling me how much money Amazon and Microsoft have made from selling these features. Since I have no interest in either of these features, I sure as hell don't care how profitable they are.

Now to social media: Facebook, Instagram, Twitter, as well as TikTok, Snapchat, and What's App. There are probably more that I've never heard of. I know and appreciate the truth that these allow people around the world to connect. It's rewarding, on the rare occasions that I find my way into Facebook, to hear news from my friend Richard in Paris. I also know that a lot of what appears online is drivel, people are obsessed by what they find on these platforms (forgive me, I had to find out from Tom they are called "platforms"). I believe that people who hang out on social media don't read many books or watch Masterpiece. But maybe they didn't anyway before TikTok.

To go back to my fantasy of life in the 1800s: on any day back then, I could master whatever I needed to know of communicating with the outside world by myself. I didn't need any help from assistants or husbands telling me how to use a piece of parchment paper to write a letter.

But I also didn't have an older brother as I have had in my true life, who having assumed that a much younger sister couldn't do anything on her own, didn't teach me but instead did everything for me. He fixed things, assembled things, understood how to make things work. I succumbed to his power and never got over it.

Ever since then I've relied on other people, alas usually men, to take care of things in certain areas for me. My assistant just set up Audible on my iPhone so I can listen to mystery novels while I ride our stationary bike. I'm grateful for that. But I tell myself I don't do any of those chores myself because I'm very good at what I'm good at, which is located mostly in my right brain, the creative area. And that I don't want to bother with the rest, some of which, to be frank, makes me anxious. I don't want to learn how to set up Spotify in my car because I like to listen to the news. I don't care about the many permutations of Google. And if my computer crashes and I lose everything I've ever written because I'm not connected to the Cloud... well, so be it.

I just wish Amazon would accept my password.

Growing Up and Away

Aunt Fritzi

The most important person in my growing-up life was neither one of my parents nor my brother. It was my Aunt Fritzi. Whoever I am today, she made me. She was my shining star, my image of what a real mother should be, as well as a real woman. She guided this impressionable child and young woman from the time I was eight years old until my early twenties, when she died. At every phase of my young life, I worshipped her.

Aunt Fritzi—her real name was Frieda Hennock—was my mother's sister, the youngest of eight children, six girls and two boys, all Russian immigrants. Like many foreigners at the beginning of the last century, they were struggling Jews who settled in New York, in the Bronx. She was six years old when she came to America and although as a young girl she spoke fluent Yiddish and Russian, she was the only one in her family who spoke English without an accent. This was crucial to me as a kid because my mother's lifelong Russian dialect was an embarrassment to me. I was forever correcting her, yearning for her to speak like my teachers and my friends' mothers. Instead of saying "already" she said "alleady" for one example, and I challenged her—"MOTHER, why can't you say it right?" I was cruel, with no patience or compassion for her inability to speak flawless English.

Aunt Fritzi, despite her limited surroundings and immigrant background, was ambitious. A gifted young pianist, she defied her father's pressure to become a musician and, when he refused to pay for her law school, she and her five sisters worked at menial jobs so that they could finance her studies at Brooklyn Law School. At twenty-three, she became the youngest woman practicing law in New York State, the first woman and first Democrat to join a prestigious New York law firm. But her renown was just beginning.

From the time I was eight years old, Fritzi would take a limo nearly every Sunday from her luxurious Park Avenue apartment to our simple home in the Long Island suburbs. I loved watching this elegant blond goddess emerge from the enormous shiny vehicle in her designer suits, her extravagant hats, and a silver fox stole slung around her neck, its face staring up at her. I would wait for her arrival, perched on the steps of our house. Some of our neighbors would walk outside when she arrived, never having seen such a huge black vehicle except at a funeral.

She adored me. I was the child she never had, the "wunderkind" who was talented at the piano as she had been and, like Fritzi, had parents who didn't fully appreciate my talents. Her mantra to me, repeated quietly at least once on every visit, was, "Don't grow up to be like your mother, you're too bright." I believed her. My mother was a mere housewife who played mahjong and canasta almost every afternoon with her friends.

I promised Aunt Fritzi I wouldn't follow my mother's dreary footsteps, and I asked if someday I could have a silver fox stole like hers. She would let me sit in the limo on the leather seats that smelled so opulent, looked so huge. Naturally, I compared it to my parents' aging Chevy.

As I got a little older, when she didn't journey out to the suburbs, she invited me to New York for weekends. I stayed in her fabulous apartment and what I remember most was her guest room with the queen-sized bed—the biggest I'd ever known—and a soft blue feather quilt. She had turned one living room window into a series of glass shelves for a dozen or so small potted plants, which she let me water and prune. She said, "These plants are yours, you can always take care of them." I always did. We called them "my children." I hated going home after these weekends.

She took me to the theatre to see the classic Broadway musicals that would much later frame my career and my life. I remember my first, *Annie Get Your Gun* with Ethel Merman. The fabulous songs, the orchestra that filled the theatre with the lush score, the bigger-than-life star with the peculiar voice. I was in heaven from the moment we walked into the theatre. I think Aunt Fritzi was, too.

We always went to the world-famous Sardi's, where I sometimes saw the celebrities whose caricatures graced the walls, and the prominent Manhattan folks who stopped by our table to hail Aunt Fritzi. She told me, "This is the most glamorous crowd in New York." Sardi's was my first experience eating lasagna, which she had to train me to pronounce correctly and which I ordered for dinner every time we dined there. It soon became my favorite food in life. It still is.

Occasionally, Aunt Fritzi took me to fancy parties where I was the only adolescent. I had a couple of dresses she had bought me, which I thought of as sophisticated. I hung on her every word and her arm, feeling shy but thrilled. We were surrounded by politicians whom I didn't recognize but I knew they were significant men. And of course, they were all men, their wives stunning arm candy. Afterward, Fritzi and I would dissect the party, her saying: "It's terrible that women aren't behaving like they're equal to men. Make sure you're always treated as an equal, or even better than the men around you." I nodded in agreement and her lectures became ingrained in my developing teenage brain.

There was another side to Aunt Fritzi. She was known as "The Blonde Bombshell" in her New York circles. I later learned that she had several affairs with prominent men who were generally married. She didn't marry until she was 52, and then to a man the whole family thought was her distinct inferior.

When I was in junior high school, Aunt Fritzi was appointed by President Harry Truman as the first female commissioner on the FCC. She was a pioneer in the fledging educational television movement, battling her six fellow commissioners as well as the forces of commercial broadcasting. She became known as an aggressive fighter, always for women's rights, education, and the Democratic Party. My mother kept a scrapbook of her press clippings, which became thick as time went by.

For several years, on into college, I would be invited to spend weekends at her sumptuous home on the Potomac, surrounded by the art and artifacts she had accumulated on her many trips to Europe. We played golf at her fancy private club, and she hosted small dinner parties honoring her amazing niece— me. She coached me beforehand on the resumes of her awesome guests. By then I could have decent conversations with them. At one of these soirees, I met Bill Simons, the man who would become her husband for only four years.

After a few years on the FCC, she was appointed to a federal judgeship, but rejected by Congress on the grounds of "personal misconduct." Oh, those affairs in Manhattan coming back to haunt her, I remember thinking when I later found out these details of her personal life. She had avoided telling me anything about this aspect of her past on her journey to mold my character and personality. It was strange learning of this part of her history which I would have loved to hear everything about, as my own sexuality was just beginning to blossom. "Why didn't I know anything about this side of your life?" I asked her. She had no answer.

Aunt Fritzi went into private law practice in D.C. until she died in 1960 of a brain tumor at the age of fifty-six. There were two funerals for her, in Washington and New York. To me, each resembled inauguration parties, given the heady populace of politicians attending. Harry Truman was there. Our whole family drove down to D.C. Her four living sisters and my brother were instructed by my mother to each bring a large suitcase. The purpose was to steal from her home as many of her antiques as possible from her despised husband. Despite my profound grief, I hooted at the sight of the black-dressed, mourning sisters, teary-eyed, shoving Fritzi's valuable *tchotchkes* into their luggage whenever Bill left the room.

I still have her elaborate silver candlesticks, which she bought on a trip to France and were stolen by my mother that day. I polish them occasionally, always recalling dear Aunt Fritzi, and keep them in a prominent spot in my living room.

My Brother

Throughout my life, I've adored my brother Martin and loathed him, been enthralled and hypnotized by him, and much of the time fearful of him. It depended on what day it was, what was his latest gambit, and what was my participation in the nuttiness. The pattern never changed until the day he died, fourteen years ago. By that time, we hadn't spoken to each other for five years.

Martin was ten years older than me, and never let me forget his dominance in size, gender, and power. When my parents brought me home from the hospital after my birth, his kingdom was forever altered, and he developed asthma almost immediately. He clung to this most transparent of ailments for the rest of his life. The early years were the days of my terror, when he and his teenage buddies would taunt me or ignore me, threaten or tease me. I followed them around, hoping for some positive attention. "Go away you little twerp," one of them shouted, and another pulled my curly hair. "Nobody wants to play with you." Martin did nothing to stop this torture. I suppose this was classic big brother/little sister stuff, but it left its mark, probably forever.

When he went off to the University of Denver, the pendulum swung for the first of dozens of times. Because he was now grown up and free, and I was stuck with my crazy mother and traveling salesman father, Martin became doting and protective. When he came home on vacation from college, bringing me books and brightly colored scarves, he told me tales of life in the grand world away from our little dull suburb. He comforted me as I became pre-pubescent, replete with tears and pimples. This sweet relationship lasted for many years, and I treasured it.

While I was in high school and he was now living in his career world in New York City, he came out to my parents' home for dinner occasionally, bringing a variety of girlfriends that had nicely sized breasts, good jobs, and clear skin. They wore high-heeled shoes and dresses that showed off real waistlines. We all had dinner around our rarely used antique mahogany dining room table, my mother nervously fussing all day on a special meal of shrimp cocktails and brisket. Did she hope Martin would marry one of these attractive dates, although he was only 24?

They were sweet to me, and I was worshipful of them, always hoping the same date would show up more than once. That didn't happen very often.

Martin reassured me I would emerge from my teenage awfulness and turn out attractive and worldly like his girlfriends. He was my adolescent zone of comfort and mature masculinity; I survived those years intact because of my brother. "You'll get out of this, you'll see," Martin repeated often. I had to believe him. He was very tall and seemed afraid of nothing.

When we were both living in New York City several years later, me in a fifth-floor walkup in Greenwich Village and he with a doorman and a real kitchen on the Upper East Side, we were friends for a while. He became rich and well-known in the city, developing a real estate project that had questionable investors. I was a '60s hippie, happily earning $75 a week doing publicity for the Mamas and the Papas. He took me to the theatre, I invited him to the Bitter End club when my bosses were performing. But as the decade progressed into the mid-'60s political dramas, I grew to feel some scorn for my Republican brother and his shallow values. When the women's movement hit—and changed my life—I shouted "sexist" to his face, and he mocked me as an "idiot".

I wasn't wise enough to avoid these conversations and the inevitable arguments that ensued. He was married by then; his wife Beverly always treaded softly with him and became a buffer between us at these times when Martin and I thought each other ridiculous and dumb. But he gave me money, which I gladly accepted and came to depend on, as it paid for a chunk of my psychotherapy.

Then Martin, Beverly, and their three small kids moved to London for his real estate business, and our sibling weirdness temporarily calmed down, given the distance between us. I visited them a few times with a boyfriend, or he took the whole family into the English countryside for a weekend. Life around Martin was exciting, extravagant.

One summer he rented a sailboat in Yugoslavia and invited me along. I was surprised at how inelegant and cramped the boat was, especially with the six passengers on board. But it was an exotic adventure. Then, through my habitual clumsiness and perhaps some latent hostility (to be discussed later with my shrink), I dropped his camera overboard on the day we landed. Martin was furious, he threw me out of his home that night. I jumped on a late train for Berlin, shattered. We didn't speak for about two years.

They had never met Tom, my most serious attachment. When we became engaged, I called Martin and Beverly in London. I told them the date we'd decided upon for the wedding, eight months hence. He said, "Can you change it? That's my busiest time of year." Controlling as always, I thought. I wouldn't succumb. We didn't alter the date, as our astrologer friend had declared it perfect. Also, I was enraged.

They didn't come to our wedding, sending a gift of a $100 check to our favorite charity. "He can be so cheap," I groaned to Tom. Again, my brother and I didn't speak for a year or more.

In the mid-'80s, they moved from London to Santa Barbara and wrote us a note wanting to mend the fragile fences. The letter, undoubtedly written by Beverly, said something like "This has gone on long enough, life is too short." Tom and Beverly acted as the peacemakers, and we drove to their home for a weekend. I was nervous and wary as we pulled into the driveway of their sprawling mansion. But it was a contented and easy time, and the beginning of a long period of solid friendship, as if all the neurotic behaviors and fits of anger we had toward each other had vanished and our advancing years had cleansed our troubled past. Martin was interested in my writing, respectful of my books and success, even read some of my articles. "I'm very impressed" was a startling bit of compliment from him.

Over the next few summers, they came with us and a group of our friends on a bike trip in France. Once we went with the whole family to Lake Tahoe for a July Fourth weekend, and Tom and I spent holidays in their guest house. We both loved the sunny, bouncy kids and Beverly became my dearest friend. I always knew she was the source of the peace, as she had learned throughout her long and difficult marriage to calm both Martin's volatility and my sensitivities to him.

In 1996 she came down with ovarian cancer, and the next eight months until her death were raw for the family. We took care of each other, we huddled, Martin and I were as close we had ever been, hugging and sharing our pain. I told Tom, "So this is what it's like to have a big brother," understanding the irony of the tragic situation.

After Beverly died, life with our family became distant again. The kids all went off to live in different areas of the country and we didn't see them much. Martin started dating some Santa Barbara "casserole ladies". In 2001, there was an episode that was like the horrid old days and marked the end of our relationship.

I had changed careers and had been working in musical theatre for a few years. I was producing *The Pajama Game* in Los Angeles for a theatre company that I had started. On a Saturday night, several friends from Chicago were in town and came to see the show, as did my brother and his girlfriend of the week. Several of us were going to late dinner afterward in a private room at a local restaurant. That morning, the *Los Angeles Times* published a scathing review of the show, the first pan I'd ever gotten. I felt depressed and humiliated. Tom begged Martin and our friends not to mention the review to me. But at dinner after the show, while our friends were eating their salads and burgers, Martin took a copy of the review from his pocket. Before he uttered a word, I was livid. Why was he carrying it around with him? He said something like, "I don't know why they said these terrible things, I thought it was good. I had a nice time." His comment engaged others to react, and a conversation ensued, with him reading bits from the review to the whole table. Furious, I grabbed Tom and we left the restaurant mid-dinner. Our friends phoned the next morning and apologized, but Martin never called. I didn't call him, and we never spoke again.

He died five years later. After he died, as I thought about his and my life together, my memories replicated the years of pain but also the happiness that spelled the arc of our long, complex relationship.

Me and My Piano

When I was six years old, our next-door neighbor, Mr. Gold, invited me to his home to play his piano. My family had no piano and I had never played before.

He was a serious amateur pianist and for some reason he offered to teach me the basics, notes, and chords. I picked it up very quickly and even learned to read music, playing the simplest of tunes appropriate for six-year-olds. I fell in love with the piano. I went next door almost every day to plunk out stuff for a few hours, probably much to the annoyance of Mrs. Gold.

Mr. Gold convinced my parents that I had a gift and they should buy me a piano, which they did. It was a Steinway grand, and it took up a good portion of our cluttered living room. My parents had no experience or interest in the piano but, like most Jewish parents, they wanted their kids to be stars. After a few years, I was playing easy classical music.

Then came Miss Brindley, my first teacher. I studied with her until I went away to college. She was a tiny woman with big teased red hair and a throaty low voice. She was always dressed up in a suit and a pearl necklace. Her teaching room was cramped, the piano filling much of the space.

My mother drove me to my weekly lessons, disappeared for an hour, then returned to take me home. I used to ask her where she went during that time and her answers were always vague. As I got older my fantasies grew, until as a hormonal teenager I imagined she was meeting a boyfriend in a funky bar in our village. It seemed strange that she never was interested in sticking around and listening to my lessons.

Miss Brindley produced occasional recitals at which all her pupils performed. She commandeered other homes for these recitals as her own space was limited, and thus we had an audience of thirty or so beaming, nervous parents. As I got older, my repertoire increased, and by the time I was a teenager I was playing Chopin etudes and the Beethoven Moonlight Sonata, the basic student repertoire. I was always told that I was exceptional; occasionally I believed it.

I was also the designated accompanist at our high school performances by student dancers and singers, and frequently played with the orchestra. I loved the attention and reveled in the music.

Meanwhile, at home my piano life was strange. At Miss Brindley's coaxing and my parents' insistence, I had to practice for an hour a day. I resented the demand and the formal structure; I was a teenager with homework, gal pals, and our crucial group activities like bra shopping and driving around looking for boys. Then too, my parents didn't appreciate the sounds of my practicing and I was forbidden from playing after my dad returned from work at 6:00, depleted. I was always baffled about the requirements and their supposed logic.

But it seemed that my future as a classical pianist was determined. I decided to go to the University of Wisconsin and major in music. Soon after I arrived, I auditioned for their artist-in-residence, Gunnar Johansen. He was a renowned Danish composer, pianist, recording artist, and lecturer, famous for replacing ailing pianists anywhere in the world, with little notice and performing at concert level. I was accepted as one of his six pupils, most of them graduate students.

The professor was a classic Dane in his looks—about six feet four, a mane of stunning silver hair, a body structure that was both slender and intimidating. He was soft-spoken but demanding, his expectations of us were high, his critiques pointed.

His other students and I sat in on each other's lessons, probably the most daunting feature of all the work with him. The graduate students were already heading down their career paths toward performing or teaching. They were focused and committed. I was a freshman at a Big Ten university, away from home for the first time, wanting to have a terrific time as well as learning. The first time I had to skip an important football game with another Big Ten school because I needed to practice piano on a Saturday afternoon, I knew there was something amiss with my life; I sensed this was perhaps not the road I should choose for my future. I was also scared much of the time, threatened by the grand professor and his other students, as well as the whole process of playing. The piano became a growing source of anxiety which became deeper than the pleasure and satisfaction.

I continued studying with Professor Johansen for two years, earned money by accompanying vocal students at their lessons. I wrote a silly musical with some friends and occasionally performed in my dorm. By the end of my sophomore year, I knew my aspirations to be a concert pianist were finished. Fear had replaced my passion. I returned to New York, went to Columbia University studying English literature, and lived with a friend in a fifth floor Greenwich Village walkup, with no piano. These were my most joyful college years.

For the rest of my life, I've usually had a piano where I lived. For the last thirty years, in my life with Tom on the beach, we've owned a Steinway grand which lives in our upstairs den. Occasionally I play, always classical works I've played in the past, usually in college. I never try to learn anything new—that's too scary—but my fingers remember the Beethoven sonatas and Chopin etudes. Sometimes I play Sondheim songs from my musical theatre books. I usually sing along if there's nobody around. The Steinway is mostly used for singing parties, at which I never play. Luckily, we have many friends that do.

When I hear or see a concert pianist perform, I am transported. I move to another realm of experience, I'm in love with the music. And I ask myself at those times, why don't I play more often, what am I afraid of? A therapist friend of mine said, "Why not just sit at the piano, don't do anything, and see what happens?" I tried that, and after fifteen or so minutes I got bored and left without playing.

A few weeks ago I went to the piano and played a Schubert impromptu which I've known for many years; in fact, I studied it with Professor Johansen. My fingers recalled about 60% of it, the rest I muddled through. I remembered how I used to play it often and vowed to go back to my piano once again. After a few moments of my playing, I noticed that my dog Roxie left the room. If only she could talk.

My Dad

When I think back to my father, he seems less present to me than either my mother or my brother. Today, I might remember him as being depressed, although I didn't know that term when I was growing up. Then, he was just quiet, calm, and predictable compared to my volatile brother Martin and my weird mother.

Dad, as I've said, was a traveling salesman, working for a small but prosperous company based in New York City that sold women's apparel. His territory was the Midwest and he was gone from home about four months of the year, trudging around cities with his sample bags. When he was back from his travels, he commuted from our small town on Long Island to his office in the city every day, a one-hour trip in each direction. He always made the 7:45 a.m. train and arrived back home at 6:00. His daily routine was that he got out of his suit and tie, put on something he called his "smoking jacket", which was a tweedy blazer, drank a large scotch and soda, and we settled down for dinner at 6:30. There wasn't much talk at our kitchen dinner table. Often we listened to the news on the radio. I think he was fatigued much of the time and made conversation only when he felt called upon.

I have a range of specific anecdotes about my dad, whom I called "Dad", as opposed to "Mother", not mom, as I addressed her. One of my favorite memories was, as a small girl, curling up next to him on his wide chaise, encircled by his arms, smelling his pipe tobacco on his sweater, feeling his warm breath. We would either nap or listen to the radio, shows like *Lux Radio Theatre* or *The Shadow* with a tag line I've never forgotten ("Who knows what evil lurks in the hearts of men? The Shadow knows.") The calm warmth of us stretched out together quieted the fear I felt so much of the time when he wasn't around. He always seemed remote but still loving, exhausted but comforting.

Then there was the only time I saw him drunk. Our neighbors across the street were Mr. Duffy and his brood of children and grandchildren, a big Irish family who had boisterous, frequent parties on their lawn. They were somehow related to a very popular radio show in the 1940s called *Duffy's Tavern*, which starred Archie the Bartender, who answered the phone bellowing, "Duffy's Tavern, where the elite meet to eat." I never understood how the show was connected to the neighbor we called Old Man Duffy (he was, in fact, old, gruff, and funny).

When Duffy died, the volunteer fire department of our little town marched with a procession of firemen in scruffy uniforms to our dead-end street, winding up at the Duffys' yard for a raucous Irish wake. All the neighbors were invited. Dad disappeared into the rowdy crowd for an hour and returned home clobbered. He was giggling, something I had never seen in my father before or since. Staggering out to our back porch to lie down on the couch he crashed through the door, shattering the glass, and wound up in the emergency room of the local hospital with a cut-up arm. It took me a while to recover from being frightened of him—anxiety was something I generated easily as a child—but it did pass. And he was my warm, peaceable dad again.

He had to record his sales figures from the trips in a giant black accounting book and I was delegated to help him. It was a task I relished and did with a mathematical precision I haven't mustered since then. I would write down the city, stores, and sales figures in the black book, working hard for perfect handwriting and accuracy. This was special. The cities and stores that he visited sounded remote and exotic. Dubuque, Waukegan, Cedar Rapids. It was so exciting for me to be a part of this routine, that I would bother him from the time he arrived home. "Dad, when are we going to work on Dubuque?" I implored, pronouncing it Du-boo-cue. He laughed at me but was touched by my willingness to do this chore.

The only time I recall seeing my dad shed tears was about his pet goldfish. He had a small pond built in our backyard, and he filled it with fish whom he called "my grandchildren." We had no dog, cat, or hamster, our only pets were the fish, for whom I cared nothing at all. But my dad fed them, cleaned the water, read the Sunday paper sitting in a beach chair next to the pond, and stared at them swimming back and forth.

One summer my brother was home from college. On a weekend night he and a buddy went out drinking, and when he returned home, they thought it would be hilarious to empty the fishpond. I was about ten, their noise woke me, I sat by my window and watched them stagger around the yard. Martin was a cruel kid, and it wasn't unlike him to do something so vicious. In the morning my father found the fish at the bottom of the empty pond, and he cried a bit, trying to hold it back. He yelled at my brother but then started all over again the next day, buying fish, cleaning the pond, filling it up with water and plants. My brother was unrepentant, my mother indifferent, but I felt my dad's sadness.

It was clear to me that my parents were not in love with each other. They would squabble for a while, then retreat into odd silences where little was spoken by either one to the other for a period of days or even weeks. Dad did not confuse marriage with happiness. Marriage meant being a responsible breadwinner and proud father, a moral man, having a good reputation in our small community, being a somewhat practicing Jew, fulfilling financial and other obligations to his wife, parents, siblings, and children. He performed what was expected of him. Whatever the passions or dreams he had locked inside him, I had no idea growing up what, if any, they were. I still don't. But I did love him, felt safe cuddling on his soft lounge chair listening to the radio together and remembering the sweet smells of his pipe on his sweater.

My Mother

B efore I knew anything about psychology, I sensed that my mother was crazy. Not the dramatic "she-should-be-locked-up-and-pumped-full-of-electricity" crazy but more of the "batty/nuts/weird not like anybody else's mother cuckoo."

My mother had many peculiar idiosyncrasies that might have arisen from her own family and her early years in troubled Russia. They came to America when she was eleven years old. She never told me much about her growing up years in New York, but I understood they were difficult.

She had deeply strange quirks. Here for example is one: In my youth I recall the magazine article she read by a doctor, touting that only hamburgers should be eaten for breakfast, no normal American breakfast food. From my age nine until I left home at eighteen, that's what I ate every morning. "It's perfect protein," she raved. "Dr. so-and-so says so." Whatever her guru's name, he had the answer to incomparable health, according to my mother. No cereal—I never had tasted oatmeal or Cream of Wheat until my dorm dining room at the University of Wisconsin—no eggs (they were reserved for dinner) and the hamburgers were always plopped onto bagels.

I was confused. I knew from sleepovers at friends' homes that bagels were reserved for cream cheese and lox, and for special occasions. But for hamburgers? And for breakfast? When Francie, my close pal, stayed overnight at our home, she glared at the breakfast table of bagels with globs of meat on top and whispered to me, "what's wrong with your mother?" I had no good answer.

Her demands frequently made no sense. Another example: When I was growing up, our living room had a sofa with big soft green pillows that was the comfiest piece of furniture in our home. My brother Martin and I argued about who would get to lie down on it to read or nap. But Mother insisted that every single one of the six pillows be puffed up and put back in its place every single time one of us got up, even if it was only for a brief journey to the kitchen or bathroom and back. If we forgot, she became visibly upset.

Then there was the nuttiness of her insisting that the staircase carpet be vacuumed by me once a day, every day, with the little hand vacuum she bought just for that purpose. But our three bedrooms were upstairs, so the stairs weren't used much during the day, and we did have a housekeeper that came twice a week. Nevertheless, for the few days in between, I was assigned to vacuum the stairs. I challenged her: "MOTHER, I CAN'T STAND DOING THIS, WHY DO YOU CARE SO MUCH?" I despised the tedium of this repetitive chore. She said, "I want them clean when I walk up the stairs, is that so hard to understand?" Yes, it was impossible to understand then and still is. I felt abused by her absurd demand; I haven't vacuumed any stairs since then.

Most Jewish mothers I knew, like my friends' mothers, wanted their boy children to become doctors, attorneys, or rich businessmen. Their ambitions for their daughters were for them to go to a good college in order to marry these substantial men, have grand homes in the New York suburbs, and to raise sons who became doctors, attorneys, or rich businessmen. Life was very predictable and certain for this generation of middle-class women.

But not my mother. Although her father was a tailor, for some inexplicable reason she had show biz in her DNA and ambitions for her son to become an actor and her daughter a classical pianist. It was not difficult for her to instill these fantasies in me. I had musical gifts and a Steinway grand piano, and I took to it quickly. With lessons from the time I was seven until I abandoned the piano at twenty,

I performed in a variety of recitals and for family gatherings. My mother sat proudly in each audience, her oversized gold hoop earrings glistening in the light. She boasted to all the other bejeweled mothers in the audience about what a fine artist I was.

This all sounds like normal parental stuff, except for one thing: my mother hated my practicing and required I do it only when she wasn't around the house, like at her afternoon canasta games with her pals. She whined many times, "it's so noisy, can't you play more quietly?" when I tried to impress her with my skill. I soon learned it wasn't the Beethoven she relished; it was the show biz.

Mother was chilly and demanding. When my father was on the road, several months a year, he called home every Sunday night. I dreaded these calls, as my mother spent most of the time complaining about me, "She doesn't help me enough around the house," and how I hadn't practiced the piano enough (how did she know? She wasn't home!). Dad never knew how to respond except to spout the requisite stern father threats to my allowance and my freedom. She dug up the same melodrama when he came home from the Midwest, and we picked him up at La Guardia Airport. She regaled him with all the things I'd done wrong while he was gone, the chores I'd ignored. He was exhausted and somewhat unresponsive. I had no rebuttal that made any difference. "OK," he whispered. "You have to be a good girl while I'm gone." He doled out some minor punishment that we both forgot about in a few days.

Mother was vain. She never wore pants or sweaters, or casual clothes, even around the house, only skirts with ruffled silk blouses, a girdle to hold up her stockings, and shoes with heels. She spent a long time putting too much rouge on her face and colored her auburn hair every six weeks. She urged me to follow her path of vanity, but I was rebellious. I didn't accept her premise that I wasn't pretty enough unless I wore ridiculous outfits and made my face look like a mask.

When I was twenty, I was anxious and depressed sometimes, between my periods of modified happiness, and I started therapy. Everybody I knew was doing it, it was a '60s craze, so it didn't seem alien to me. But my mother was horrified when I told her, especially when I asked her to pay for the part that my brother wasn't picking up. The doctor had told me, "I don't know if your mother is crazy—whatever that means—but her oddities certainly helped form some of your issues." Shrink talk. But on the nose.

Mother was shocked that I was talking about my parents to a stranger, and she quizzed me relentlessly in phone calls about what did I say and what did he say. I wouldn't tell her. "Mother," I insisted, "these are private conversations. And they're helping me a lot." She was skeptical. After several months of my therapy, she sent me a book called *Don't Blame Your Parents*, the subject and tone matching the title. For the year or so that I spent with this therapist, I blamed my mother for everything that was wrong in my young life.

Eventually, I developed compassion, if not love, for this unhappy, unsatisfied, strange woman. And then she sued me.

My Mother Sued Me

Yes, you read that correctly. She was offended by something I wrote about her marriage in my book that was being published, and she engaged my uncle Harold, a prominent attorney in New York, to sue me and my publisher, Random House, while my book, *Options: A Personal Expedition Through the Sexual Frontier*, was still in manuscript form. My editor told me he'd never had this bizarre experience of being sued by an author's parent.

I was mortified. Why on earth would she do this, I thought, reading and re-reading the chapter, trying to understand her rage. I'd written about her several times before, and she'd always relished being in print, especially if I used her name, Paula. What I wrote about her was irrelevant. She merely cherished the celebrity of it all. She would tell all her friends about her brilliant daughter, the writer. She never saw the underpinnings in what I wrote that included her many idiosyncrasies. She never felt offended, even when I occasionally referred to her unsatisfying marriage. But this time was very different.

I thought that my mother might be somewhat upset by what I'd written in that new book in a chapter on the genesis of marriage. The first sentence of this section was: "My own parents, like most others I saw, were not happy together." From there, I guessed it spiraled downhill, as I wrote of her disappointment in her marriage, "...the anger hardening into turgid knots over the years." Then it spoke of her early fantasies for a romantic, glamorous relationship in which she and my dad would dine out and go dancing once a week. This dream contrasted with my father's middle-class values, his weariness as a traveling salesman, and I knew that it never happened as she had fantasized. This entire portion of the 285-page book was only two pages long.

My brother Martin and I were in Miami Beach where my widowed mother lived, several months before the publication of the book, planning to show her the pages in this early manuscript state, to temper whatever feelings of exposure she might have. She talked frequently about her forty-two-year marital misery to anyone who even pretended to listen, and I figured whatever objections she had would vanish after seeing herself in print, as well as eating the lush apple pie we brought to her apartment for dessert. At first, she was thrilled to see us. She said she was honored to have the rare occasion to have us together; at that time Martin lived in London and I in Los Angeles. He was vacationing in Florida with his family for the summer; I flew in for a visit and this conversation.

Her home was a condo in a large building near the beach, its population exclusively retirees, usually from some other state, often widows. Her living room was sunny and pleasant, all the upholstered chairs and sofa covered in the same soft blue and white floral fabric. Dinner was her renowned creation of pot roast and potato pancakes. She was decked out in her trusty polyester pants and a bold striped blouse. She wore the substantial amount of face makeup that I recalled from my childhood and her usual oversized earrings that appeared to match her blouse. The visit promised to my brother and me to be familiar and unthreatening. What could go wrong?

I gave her the manuscript pages to read. She wailed after reading the entire two pages. "How could you say these things?" "What will all my friends think?" "But, MOTHER," I bellowed, "you tell anyone and everyone about Dad and what a terrible husband he was." I was startled and felt maligned.

She had told the world that she could have married the early movie star Fredric March. (I always thought that would be a terrific title for a book about my mother, *I Could Have Married Fredric March*.)

The truth, as it turns out, was that as a young girl she worked at her father's dry cleaners in the Bronx where the actor used to bring his clothes, and she developed a crush, an elaborate fantasy about his proposing to her. At moments when she was most depressed in her marriage, she recalled this delusion. I'm sure it only made my father look worse in her eyes. Fredric March would certainly have taken her dancing once a week.

Mother left the living room for a few minutes, I guess to gather her thoughts. Martin, who had an extra decade with my mother, was even more appalled than I was. "What on earth is she so upset about?" he said. "I thought she would have printed this chapter in the condo newsletter." I answered, "I don't understand her. With my other books, she was so proud she'd go into bookstores and announce she was my mother and when nobody was around, she'd change the display, so my book was placed in front of the others on the shelves."

When Mother returned to the dining room, pulling herself up to her grand five foot three, grasping her amber necklace with both hands, she declared, "I only hope I'm dead when this book comes out." She then marched from the room again. Martin and I were flabbergasted, had no idea how to respond. She was gone from the room for about fifteen very long minutes. When she returned, even more upset, I did manage to say something like, "I'm sorry you feel that way," realizing how inadequate that sounded. We bolted right away, and I left Miami the next day. Mother wouldn't speak to either of us for several weeks.

After we left, apparently she called my Uncle Harold in New York and set the legal wheels in motion. A few days later my editor, embarrassed but resolute, called and told me I had to lighten up the two pages or they would not publish the book. They would not risk a lawsuit. I made enough changes to satisfy Mother, of course. The book was published six months later. My mother never mentioned my book again.

Boys, Boys, and No Boys

I was not a popular girl with boys in my adolescent years. I was shy, chubby, and had frizzy blond hair. I had lots of girlfriends, but we were never the "A" group, we were the smart ones with the good grades, but were considered the "B" group by the boys I was attracted to.

There was one boy I was madly in love with from seventh grade all the way through high school: Jeremy Grant. He was very handsome, muscular, fairly stupid, and for all those years didn't know I existed. I did everything I could in my tiny repertoire of tricks to get his attention: I maneuvered to secure a desk close to him in classes we were in together; at football games (of course he was on the team) I cheered myself hoarse whenever he made the simplest move on the field. I became the piano accompanist for all the high school theatre and dance concerts—a fine accomplishment which I achieved hoping that Jeremy Grant would notice me on the stage performing brilliantly. Nothing worked.

What does it say about me that when I was old enough to drive, I got all dressed up, I borrowed my mother's car and drove to Jeremy's home, about eight blocks away from ours, parked across the street, and just waited in the car, staring at his windows? I was convinced he would come outside while I spent about an hour doing secret stalking. My plan was that as soon as I saw him exit, I would jump out of the car, run up to him, and, with enormous enthusiasm, flirtatiousness, and sophistication, have a fabulous conversation.

I planned everything I would say, knowing it would, at last, turn him on to me. He would ask me out and we would soon be going steady, his class ring around my neck. I did this bizarre secret routine twice a week at least, for a year, and he never came out of his house. Ever. My fantasies about Jeremy didn't end until I traveled across the country to study piano at the University of Wisconsin, and he went to work in his father's auto repair shop.

Going back in time to public school: We lived on a small dead-end street. At the far corner, Danny and Peter Phillips lived. We played together with my crew of gal pals throughout public school, Danny in my class and Peter a year older. They were ruffians, pulled our hair and our skirts, but we loved the attention, we felt desired. Our mothers played canasta together once a week.

One day, the boys arrived at my backyard with thick brown twine and tied me up, both laughing ominously, while I just stood there frightened to death. The ropes hurt, but I didn't know what to make of it, what kind of new game they were creating. When Peter announced, "we're going to set you on fire," pulling out a box of kitchen matches, I shrieked "STOP, WHAT ARE YOU DOING?" My dad heard me from inside our house, ran outside, and seeing me bound up, grabbed Peter's arm. He twisted it so hard it resulted in a severe sprain, Danny bellowed an ear-splitting scream, and both boys bolted down the street, leaving my father to untie and hold me while I wept. My friendship with the boys was over, my mother's canasta games with their mother were finished, the families never spoke again.

Here's the worst part of the story: The boys' father was the only dermatologist in our town, so when I was a pimply teenager I had no expert to help me with my adolescent face.

I didn't go to my Junior Prom, neither did any of my girlfriend gang of seven. Nobody asked us. We spent the night together at a pajama party in my home, overeating and gossiping, giving each other facials, and pretending we didn't feel sorry for ourselves. As I said, we were the "B" list in high school terms: good grades, active in after-school events, sporty. However, we were not the cheerleaders.

But the Senior Prom for me was a magical experience. Through my mother, I was "fixed up" on a blind date with Bob Krasner who had just finished his freshman year at Harvard. "Harvard, oh my God," I told myself. And he was a year older than me, a real man. I was off to Wisconsin in the Fall, had left my high school boy traumas pretty much behind me. My mother bought me a strapless lavender tulle gown and high-heeled shoes which we had dyed to match. I was nervous as hell.

Bob was very attractive and somewhat Harvard-pretentious. He was an English major and he quoted authors I'd never read, like James Joyce and William Faulkner, during the drive to my high school gym. He was impressed I was going to study piano, which none of my high school male comrades seemed to notice. He was also a clumsy dancer, but I didn't care. I was at my Senior Prom with a curly-haired Harvard man. What could be better? My girlfriends were impressed, I introduced him to some of the "B" boys, but Jeremy Grant still didn't notice that I existed.

On the way home, he found a parking lot somewhere and we started to neck. I had had only brief experiences with kissing boys and never with anyone who knew what they were doing. I assumed he did. But I was perplexed: He gave me my very first soul kisses and I didn't like them much, they were very long and gloppy. He said to me at some point in the exercise: "Are you hot yet?" I had no idea how to respond, and I wasn't hot yet. I didn't really know what "hot" was. "I'm sorry, I just don't know," I answered. He looked hurt. But I was still caught up in the incomparable magic of my prom. We saw each other a few times after that night, our "sex life" didn't improve but I read *The Sound and the Fury* before our second date and we discussed it deeply.

Then I was off to college and an entirely new life. I never went back to my hometown as my parents had moved away and my girl buddies had also left. I have no idea what happened to Jeremy Grant, Bob Krasner, and the monster Phillips boys.

My Greenwich Village Apartment

My friend Sheila and I had lived in the same dorm—Hampton House—for two years at the University of Wisconsin. Then we both left and moved back to Manhattan to finish our last two years of college. We were New York kids, having grown up in two different but similar Long Island suburbs, small and boring, with one movie theatre in each town and not much else to do.

I had spent as much time as parental guidance had allowed in the city during my high school years, and I was in love with New York, of course. I went with family members who lived there—like my beloved Aunt Fritzi—or my mother, to the theatre, the opera, concerts at Carnegie Hall, and shopping at Macy's.

Sheila and I spent much of our time in Madison, Wisconsin dreaming of transferring out of this dreary town, away from this hokey midwestern college population, these silly fraternity parties where the beer overflowed, frequently onto the floor. We wanted fabulous Manhattan.

So, we both transferred after our sophomore year, Sheila to New York University to study fashion and I to Columbia University as an English lit major, to read the great works of contemporary literature. Somehow, I'm not sure how, we both convinced our parents to let us get an apartment together.

My first apartment was a funky fifth-floor walkup in an old brownstone at 81 Perry Street in the middle of Greenwich Village, right off the shopping and coffeehouse mecca of Bleecker Street. I was lucky that my mother couldn't manage the flights of steep stairs, so she never saw our dwelling in the two years that I lived there, until Sheila got engaged and moved out. I'll describe the apartment, which I cherished so much I can remember all the details to this day.

It was a furnished railroad apartment. That is, it had one hallway with all the rooms leading off the hall. Except they weren't separate rooms with doors, they were just spaces. There weren't many spaces. You entered through the front door into the small kitchen and hopefully didn't stumble over the bathtub which lived there, right outside the bathroom door. Then you followed the hallway past an open space with a single bed, one dresser for the two of us, and one closet. Then you continued walking on past the only bedroom, which had a double bed but no door, only a slim yellow curtain to separate it from the hall. Then on to the living room, a sweet room with a no-kidding real fireplace, a large decorative mirror above it, and windows looking out onto our exotic Perry Street.

There was no privacy, no rooms to retreat into and no doors to hide behind. Sheila and I traded sleeping places every week so one of us would have a slightly larger bed. We each cleaned up the place often and struggled to stay neat in a space barely acceptable for one tenant, much less two.

The rent was $85 a month.

We were happier than either of us had ever been. We lived two blocks away from the White Horse Tavern where we went for beers a few times a week and sometimes were picked up by Beatnik boys. Sometimes one of us would bring a scruffy-haired hero home to neck in the living room. The other one of us would either hide in a local coffee shop for an hour or so or stay at the White Horse and drink more beer. There was no privacy in our apartment. We agreed our necking sessions wouldn't last more than an hour, which was plenty of sex time since we weren't going any further in those years.

I remember a dirty old man who lived on the third floor, and he was extremely dirty. He came out of his door when he heard my footsteps on the stairs and glared at me as I walked up or down. He never spoke. And I was too frightened to confront him.

Then there was the small grocery store on the corner where we bought most of our food supplies. At the deli counter they sold chicken skins, separated from the rest of the chickens. They lived in their own vat, golden and crispy. I often bought the skins for dinner, along with the mushy potato salad. We hardly ever cooked, occasionally a cheesy omelet.

In Washington Square we listened to folk music guitars and carried hand-made signs protesting the building of luxury apartments in the neighborhood; we heard Miriam Makeba and Bob Dylan sing at The Bitter End; we went to poetry readings at The Gaslight Café on MacDougal Street; we saw Lenny Bruce at the Village Vanguard and esoteric plays at The Cherry Lane Theatre. I took guitar lessons from Dave Van Ronk, a star folk singer, in his apartment, where his wife often walked around topless.

Commuting was easy for Sheila; she merely walked about seven blocks to NYU. I had to take a forty-minute subway ride uptown to Columbia, which felt like it was in another country from the Village. Never mind, I didn't care. I wouldn't have lived anywhere else. I was in the center of the universe.

My Abortions

I lost my virginity at the age of twenty-one, in the early 1960s, and got pregnant that night. My boyfriend of two years was Larry B., who owned a second-hand furniture store on Long Island, outside of New York City. We did freshmen sex activities for the whole relationship, which seemed right to me. Having actual intercourse was something that none of my girlfriends did at that time, and Larry didn't promote it. In fact, I suspected he was getting it somewhere else. Of course I cared, but I just didn't want to abandon my virginity.

As I look back, given the gargantuan changes in the culture since the early 1960s, I can't remember why I was adamant about maintaining my status as a virgin, but there it was. I was "hip" in many ways, just not in that one. And abortions were illegal, that's the main point in all of this.

One night Larry and I were alone in my apartment in Manhattan. We had a few rye and ginger ales, the cocktail of the time, started to fool around, our clothes came off and then it seemed that the natural thing to do was to "go all the way". That's what it was called in those days. Going all the way.

Afterward, I was surprised and disappointed that the experience itself wasn't more like what romance novels proclaimed and that I didn't feel any different. I didn't have rosy cheeks or the sense of being wildly in love. I hadn't had an orgasm. I was the same old me.

I didn't see Larry for a few weeks after that non-earth-shattering night, which was typical of our relationship. When I didn't get my period on schedule, I went to the doctor and found out the truly earth-shattering news that I was pregnant.

Larry vanished after I told him the news. I never saw or spoke to him again.

Of course, I would have an illegal abortion, there was no other route for me. At that time, it wasn't difficult to find people who performed abortions. You could travel to Puerto Rico for one, or northern Pennsylvania for another, and you knew the abortionists' names. In New York City there were dozens of available practitioners.

My girlfriends were kind and solicitous, I also turned to my brother Martin to take care of me and give me money to pay for it. Martin, who was protective and also vindictive, wanted to drive out to Larry's home in the suburbs and pour sugar in his car's gas tank, thus destroying the engine. I supported the plan, as I was not above desiring revenge for his abandonment of me. But soon I felt that I'd had such devastating luck getting pregnant my first time out with sex—whoever heard of such a thing?—that I would probably have the same dreadful fortune with the gas tank, and I made Martin cancel the project.

I found an abortionist. His fee was $1,000 in cash, a fortune in those years. Martin paid for it.

My roommate Lois took me for the abortion. It was in a seedy brownstone building on the Lower East Side. A woman in a face mask answered the door and made Lois wait outside. When I was taken inside, I was immediately blindfolded. I never saw the apartment, the room in which the procedure took place, or the doctor's face. I only remember his harsh voice, my terror, and the blackness of not seeing anything. Everything else was a blur afterward except for a small amount of blood and pain and being ushered outside where the blindfold was removed. Lois got a taxi to take us home.

I spent the next two days in bed, sleeping and feeling relieved that it was all over. I left a nasty message on Larry B's answering machine, but he never responded.

I didn't have a sense of having killed a potential child, a feeling of shame. I had no reality of regret or guilt. Only relief. The feelings of terror left me quickly, but never the memory of that horrific morning and the blindfold. Still, on the occasion I'm in New York and happen to pass that broken-down building, after all these decades, it comes back to me in a flash, and the emotions return for a few dark moments.

I became a passionate activist on behalf of legal abortion, a woman's right to choose her own path, and in 1973, twelve years later, I celebrated, along with all the women I knew, the passage of *Roe v. Wade*. It was one of the monumental moments of my life.

In 1976, I was living with Mark P. in Los Angeles. It was a solid relationship. Then I became pregnant. He had two teenage kids, didn't want any more, nor did I have any interest in being a mother. It was predictable that I would end the accidental pregnancy.

The experience couldn't have been more of a profound opposite than the illegal abortion. I went to my gynecologist, a gray-haired kindly Beverly Hills physician who performed the procedure. It was so comfortable that it felt almost like having any other regular office routine. Mark took me home, I slept for a few hours, and that night we went to our favorite Italian restaurant for pasta and prosecco. It was over. I had no residual feelings of humiliation or regret. Nor did he.

The current nightmare began in August, 2021 when in Texas abortion was declared illegal, the

Supreme Court refused to challenge their new law, many states went along with it or even expanded it and now in 2022 *Roe v. Wade* has been overturned. It's impossible to predict where this will end. Forms of contraception illegal? Same sex marriage gone? No morning after pill? No more IUDs? Oral sex gone?

My brain is flooded with pictures of women having to take the illegal journey, being blindfolded in Louisiana apartments, or traveling out of state if they can even afford it. Recently, I had a dream about my first abortion of so many years ago. The memories came rushing back in nightmare form. I ask myself, several times a day, how on earth could this be happening NOW, in America, after all these decades? What about our privacy rights? And what can I do about it? What can we all do? What WILL I do?

The Women's Movement: New Direction

It was 1968. I had marched up Fifth Avenue, picketed, bussed to D.C., shouted, had fights with family and friends. I was then working in book publishing, where I was first the Publicity Director at New American Library and then at Dell. These publishing companies were bastions of liberal and left-wing values. And of course, they were run by men. Doing publicity for pushy and often horny authors was about as high up the corporate ladder as my female cohorts and I could climb. The workplace was still in the Mad Men era.

It was the early days of the movement. *MS Magazine* wouldn't be born for another four years, *Roe v.*

Wade didn't pass for five more. My friends and I were all hanging out with other women, which became increasingly satisfying as well as natural and crucial to our well-being. The term "Consciousness-Raising" entered and consumed our vocabularies.

So, in the fall of '68, seven pals and I started a Consciousness-Raising or "CR" group, one of dozens gathering around the city. We met every Tuesday night at a different member's apartment. We were powerful independent women, more or less success-ful, some married or living with men, some—like myself—single and dating. All our situations would alter dramatically during the three years we were banded together. The Women's Movement was burst-ing and challenging lives all over the place.

For my friends and myself, what was primarily raised in our consciousness was a level of anger at men that was new, shocking, and global. If I read a piece in The New York Times about, say, some politician, what would escalate my pulse would be a condescending remark he made about a woman that previously I wouldn't have noticed but now re-ally pissed me off. I'd bring the article to our next meeting; almost everyone would have seen it, (it was The New York Times after all), and we each had something strong to say, our voices getting more strident as the discussion intensified. Many people outside of our realm thought feminism equaled man-hating. I think for some time until we got our bearings, took ourselves seriously, and were taken seriously, they were probably right.

The side effects of our group ranged from dramatic—one marriage dissolved—to symbolic. Example: the more radical women stopped shaving their legs, armpits, and tweezing their eyebrows. Why should we go to all that trouble when men didn't? I never went that far myself, although I did admire the gesture.

I noticed that for the married women, their husbands always left home for the evening before our group arrived. I always wondered where they went for all those hours. Who amongst their men pals were gathering and what were they gabbing about? I was sure I knew.

Ah yes, what happened to our connections with the men in our lives? My boss at Dell Publishing, Walter T., was a somber and wimpy sort of fellow. I had to confront him every day about his dismissive treatment of me and the other women in the office. Thank goodness, he also wouldn't have known how to hit on me, even in the unlikely case that he wanted to.

The guys who were moving through my dating life more rapidly than ever before became terrified of me and turned off. What happened to that charming, seductive, and unthreatening Marcia? Who is this new woman who's not so easy these days to lure into bed? And not so passive and compliant if she got there? They left quickly, except for the rare man who appreciated and understood the transformation that was occurring within me and so many women in New York.

So, it was fury that surged through my friends and me much of the time. But not only that. My increasing sense of strength, of true independence, my value, altered me permanently. I participated in women's political agendas, left publishing, and became a journalist. I wrote magazine pieces about our changing lives, and I continued marching. I worked on researching my first book, *The Eternal Bliss Machine: America's Way Of Wedding*.

In the Fall of 1971, I moved to Los Angeles. I had spent the previous two winters there, writing various articles for newspapers and magazines. I cherished the weather, the ocean, and the slower, relaxed pace of life. When I made the permanent move from New York, my plan was to write my book in peace, a state of being not accessible to me in Manhattan.

I rented a small house in the Hollywood Hills, rescued a peculiar dog, and dug in to write. I even acquired a boyfriend, an actor I'll call Danny G, who wore medical coats instead of sports jackets and was totally aligned with the women's explosion. He supported everything I did. He was easy for me to be with.

The difference between LA and New York was the surprising lack of women's activities, particularly the CR groups. As far as I could tell from asking my few girlfriends, there were none. I felt the need to start one.

So, one night I invited six women to my home, hoping it would replicate my New York clan that had transformed my life. I was utterly shocked when twenty-eight women showed up at 7:30. The word had gotten around via my friends, and the hunger for female community was clearly immense. The women came from all over the city, they were curious and excited. Crowded into my few rooms, they broke into small clusters. We created a single discussion topic for all, something like "what's missing from your life as a woman", and they talked for hours, sharing candidly with these welcoming strangers. I walked from room to room, checking in on each conversation, deeply moved by the openness and yearning for connection that I saw in each gathering.

The CR groups continued meeting, some lasted for several years, including the one I joined that evening. Women changed, their lives altered, sometimes their family patterns were disrupted or crashed. That was the inevitable cost of what was, and still is a revolution.

One night I was at a party in Santa Monica, given by a married friend, a woman in my group. Her husband, whom I had met once before, walked over to me and said: "You came to Los Angeles and you ruined my life." He turned away; those were the last words he ever spoke to me. I knew exactly what he meant, of course.

Money, the Root of So Much

When I was a kid, growing up in Rockville Center, a suburb of New York City, I didn't think about money very much. Whether my father earned a lot, or whether our home was more or less opulent than my friends' homes was of no concern to me. My parents never discussed our finances.

Then one day my brother Martin came home for some holiday with a joke gift: a framed cover of the notable *Life Magazine* with a photo of my father's face, and a headline that said, "The richest man in Rockville Center earns $100,000 a year." He hung it in the hall, next to the front door, so everyone could see it as they entered the house.

I thought it was real, of course, even though the family hooted when the picture was unwrapped. I didn't remember that when, at about age twelve, I had asked my dad how much he earned; he said he made $30,000 a year, which had us be what he called "comfortable."

Suddenly things changed in my head when I believed we were rich: I wanted more and better clothes, I wanted a new fancier bike, I wanted a pedigree dog, I wanted us to have a bigger TV. None of this happened. I started comparing my home with my friends' homes, our car with theirs—although I knew nothing about cars. I started measuring everything on a money scale. I went through my teenage years worrying about money for the first time, totally puzzled by what it meant.

Cut to: 1973 in Los Angeles, where I now lived, scraping by as a neophyte journalist, working constantly but earning south of $25,000 a year. I spent three years researching and writing my first book. By the end of that scenario, I was utterly broke, living in a dumpy house in the Hollywood Hills, driving a rented used Chevy and scraping by, with occasional gifts from my brother who always lectured me that I should get a real job. I could tell he resented every minor check he wrote, believing I should be completely independent or find a husband who would support me.

Then one day the paperback rights to the book sold for a nifty six-figure sum. I had no idea what to do with it, or how to manage it. Luckily, an ex-boyfriend who was a financial manager in the movie business offered to guide me. On his advice, I bought a charming Spanish-style home with a pool in the Hollywood Hills, a snappy red Fiat convertible, and took a two-month trip to Europe. I found someone who took care of investments for me. Best of all, I no longer had to scrounge money from my family. My image of myself as a poor struggling journalist altered overnight.

Everything changed in my relationship to money—my sense of myself, my relationship with some friends, my needs. And it wasn't all for the better. I wondered if I was supposed to pick up the check when I went to a restaurant with a friend or two; sometimes I distrusted if a guy was interested in me or my money; how much should I spend on that cashmere sweater or should I even be buying cashmere at all? I wondered if I should pretend I was still struggling. Will I run out of funds if I don't have another windfall or don't find a rich man? Could I now love a poor guy? I had no understanding of how having money would affect my life. In fact, the subject was much more puzzling than in the old days when I was obsessed with how much I had in my checking account.

Today, decades later and comfortably married, I'm still tempted to buy the string beans on sale, even if they're two days old and somewhat wilted. I fret about Tom's spending habits compared to my thriftiness. Both of our incomes are inconsistent and unpredictable, his significantly larger than mine. But I seem to bear the burden of worry for the two of us. Probably, neither of us has a realistic sense of how we're doing. I can't tell if he truly isn't concerned about money, confident that we're always ok, or if he's just saying that to placate my inherent nervousness. I asked him about this recently, and he answered that he's never worried about money, always confident we have enough. He doesn't think he's extravagant, and of course I do, but what he says is that it's there to give us pleasure. I envy his cool. I turn off all the lights when we're going out for the evening.

Meanwhile, If the wild Alaskan salmon at the market is too expensive—and my brain needs to somehow compute what that means—I'll usually settle for the much cheaper tilapia, even though I don't relish it as well. I notice my varying attitudes about money remind me of being an acrobat between trapezes. I am only hoping there is a net under me.

No Kids, Thank You

I have never wanted kids. It might be because I grew up in such a wacky family. It could be that I always wanted a career instead. It also might be that, as a young woman, when I observed my friends and their children it wasn't an appealing sight. It could simply be that I've never found children very interesting. My friends view me as a loving wife and cherished pal. I think I am. My decision not to be a mother goes back to my childhood.

My family, specifically my mother and brother, were nuts, as I've described. It wasn't a loving safe nest in which to grow and flourish, it was a dark and scary place. You could argue that "Yes, but wouldn't that give you a motive to create the opposite environment for children?" My brother had three kids, I had various friends who didn't have happy early families but still wanted kids. But I never yearned for them, I worried I would expose them to something less than perfect in myself. I didn't have any conflict about this choice.

By the time I met and married Tom, I was forty-two, he had raised two boys while living with their mother for many years. He didn't enjoy the experience, and on our second date we agreed that neither of us wanted children. It was an enormous relief, and I then knew we could move forward together.

I always wanted and have had a career and various charity activities, none of them consistent with building a family. Living in New York City in my twenties, I had a life of glamorous jobs that paid almost nothing but filled me with a sense of my own cosmopolitan sophistication. I did publicity for a small movie company on a film that was just being released, I worked for a restaurant conglomerate and gained fifteen pounds in three months from taking clients to fancy lunches; I was publicity director for Dell and New American Library publishing companies and accompanied authors on their book tours. I was PR head for Electra Records and became a lifelong folk music fanatic. There was no space or desire to even think about having children.

I threw myself into the birth of the 1960's Women's Movement, I had endless conversations about how marriage and family life were dead, a betrayal of women. I was shocked when a great pal of mine, a leading feminist, had twins. And they were boys! How on earth would she be able to raise boys in this world?

In the late '60s, I began to write pieces for magazines and newspapers, and my career as a journalist flourished for over twenty years. I moved to Los Angeles to write my first book and stayed. Nowhere in my life, as I waltzed through my thirties, was there room or a need for children. I wanted to marry someday, but it would have to be with someone who felt as I did about not creating a family.

Many of my girlfriends got married and had kids. When I visited, I thought the infants and toddlers were adorable and I would attempt to give them my attention, but my behaviors always felt dumb and useless. When they were old enough and started to shriek, they lost me forever. I said to Tom just last week, "why do children scream so much, can't they just speak in normal tones?" He had no specific answer, even though he's trained as a psychologist. He explained, in general, that they're either scared or excited. We hear them on the beach wailing for no apparent reason; their parents look like they want to either collapse with exhaustion or commit murder.

A gay friend asked me today if I felt I had to justify not having children. He said that he did, he had to explain himself and his choices to people. I did not. Except once, when a friend who was Orthodox Jewish and straddled with four kids said, "Do you feel guilty, or selfish?" I thought about her question for less than a minute and answered: "I don't feel guilty at all, and I think being selfish is okay, since it's my life to do with what I want."

I have never found kids interesting to be around. I don't find their behaviors cute or fascinating or brilliant, their self-centeredness appealing, and I can't bear their crying. By the time I want to interact with them, they are at least fifteen and must be quite smart. My grandnephew, at sixteen, has recently declared himself "sexually fluid", has changed his name from Jake to Jackie, and talks to me openly about the vast complexities of this new world of gender identification. I find him thoroughly engaging.

As a mother, I'm very sure I would be obsessed with every moment of my child's behavior, I would worry about all things huge and tiny, always be fatigued, and feel the impingement on my time and my brain constantly. A few days ago, I was settling down on our living room couch with delicious time and space to dig into a new novel, when I had this thought: "What if I had a child right now who clamored for my attention and I had to abandon this perfect few hours to get involved in some tedious activity? If I said, "No dear heart, come back in two hours, mommy is reading a book," little Chauncey would weep and stomp away and I'd feel that I had ruined his life. My wondrous private hours with my novel would be finished, as would my self-esteem. Guilt would overwhelm me.

I guess it would be terrific to be a grandmother. My friend Helen has four grandkids, two of whom visit her each Saturday. She adores them and the whole weekly experience. Much more, she admits, than being a mom. "With kids", she says, "I couldn't wait until dinner was over and they would go to bed. I was always worrying about what impact I was having on them. But with my grandchildren, I can just have a great time. I have the freedom to really engage with them, see how their brains work. A parent has so much to juggle, but these kids are always fun, and then they go home."

I am a nutty dog person; I believe that's my version of having children. I am devoted to most dogs, whether mine or somebody else's. But I can guess from my thoughts and behavior towards Roxie, my adored mutt, what kind of flawed and compulsive mother I would be. I've sometimes asked Tom, "Do you think Roxie is happy?", worried about whether I could be providing her a better life. Like if we lived on a huge ranch and she could cavort wildly every day, not on a leash, not with any human controlling her movements. Wouldn't she be in bliss every day?

He assures me, while giving me an odd look, that she's perfectly content. She curls up in a little bed next to me while I'm at my desk, and if I've been there for several hours I wonder, with some guilt, if she's bored. I know dogs are supposed to sleep about 12 hours a day, but nonetheless, I'm guilty. Am I feeding her the perfect food for her health, providing her sufficient exercise, scratching her belly enough so she feels loved? Am I crazy?

The world is better because I've never had children. And, obviously, so am I.

Adventures and
Close Encounters

Chasing Mother Teresa

I first flew from New York to Calcutta, but Mother Teresa had left the day before to handle an emergency in Bangladesh. I jumped on a plane, but she was just leaving for Kathmandu, Nepal, to deal with another crisis. Then, with almost no sleep in several days, I flew to Nepal, over Mt. Everest, where I felt like leaping from the tiny, bouncing Indian Airlines plane onto the world's deadliest mountain and putting an end to this fruitless project. By the time I got to Kathmandu, she had once again just left.

I was traveling with my colleague and friend, Nathan Gray, who was an executive at Oxfam International in Boston and a third-world adventurer.

He had met Mother Teresa when he went to India to help when an earthquake struck a few years before. He had called me one day with a bizarre idea: Would *Playboy Magazine*, where I'd written several long, intense Interviews with famous folks, be interested in an Interview with Mother Teresa, and if so, would they pay for the trip for both of us? Of course, I called *Playboy* immediately, heart racing, and my editor agreed to send us. And then the good lady's staff of nuns, not exactly understanding what *Playboy* was, welcomed the idea.

In those years, pre-computer ease, making a plane reservation in India meant we had to sit in the airline's office for many hours surrounded by the endless line of travelers, while the clerks phoned and talked to human beings who had to phone other human beings to make a simple reservation. Our scurrying around the Indian sub-continent in the hunt for Mother Teresa was a huge and complicated task, not made any easier by the belly problems we were both having. Nonetheless, we forged ahead.

While we were waiting to hear where we would possibly find her, I decided to fly to New Delhi to meet with *The New York Times* bureau chief, who had interviewed her several times over the past few years. He was a tough, worldly journalist and what he told me over lunch about his time with Mother Teresa stunned me. He said that being in her presence so profoundly moved him, that he was considering giving up his amazing job, his Judaism, moving his family to Calcutta, and going to work for her.

After three weeks of traveling through India, we all finally connected in Calcutta, her home base and one of the poorest cities in the world. It was also one of the most crowded, with hordes of citizens stationed on every street, making walking anywhere difficult. Calcutta had all the qualities of a poverty-ridden metropolis of ten million people. I wondered why Mother Teresa chose this desperate city for her home base until her nuns took us to the Home for the Destitute and Dying, a dilapidated building overcrowded with ill and aged people in beds, which was run and funded by her worldwide group, the Missionaries of Charity.

I then understood that she was completely dedicated to helping where no one else would, to caring for the neediest among us and that Calcutta was the perfect place for her to follow her life's path. Walking through the building was an overwhelming experience for both Nathan and me, one that we were anxious to leave behind after an hour. We felt guilty but were relieved stretching out by the small pool at our hotel.

The next day I finally met Mother Teresa at her office. The space also served as a home and school for abandoned children. When she walked into the reception room, in her blue and white sari, surrounded by her staff of four nuns, I was surprised at how tiny she was, how frail she looked. She sat next to me at the table and stared deeply into my eyes before saying anything. Her English was good, her sentences short and pointed. She was warm but clearly distant. I had the sense that much of what she said had been rehearsed or spoken before to journalists in precisely the same words. Oddly, I wanted to touch her, to hold her hand, but in her sweet manner, she rebuffed any physical contact. The wall around her was clear and uncrossable. I didn't comprehend the feelings I was having for her from the very first moment, they were not simple or easily understood.

The interview went well, she didn't object to the tape recorder, and she was focused. Finally, I had to ask her the tricky question about abortion. In this overpopulated, poverty-ridden city, how did she explain her anti-abortion stance? Her exact words stayed with me until today: "Bring all the unwanted children to me, I will take care of them." She had nothing else to say on the subject. Children were left at her front door, many ill, deformed, all discarded by their families. She took them all in, gave them a home, educated them, loved them for years.

After three hours, she signaled me that the interview was over. By then I knew in my heart, mind, and body, that Mother Teresa was a saint—whatever that is. I wasn't sure, I'm still not, but I know I had never had that experience before or since. When I returned to the hotel, I was teary all day, I missed her and, dare I say it—I loved her. Like the New York Times journalist, I thought for an hour about giving up my wonderful life in America to be with Mother Teresa in Calcutta. My friend Nathan explored adopting one of her orphans, an infant with only one arm, and bringing him home to Boston. I convinced him his wife and kids might be shocked when they picked him up at the airport. He finally relented. So did I.

I never had enough time with her or got sufficient candid responses to my tough questions to write the *Playboy* Interview. But what I've been left with, after all these years, is the overpowering reality that I had been in the presence of a saint. She died in 1997, eighteen years after I was with her, and in 2016, Mother Teresa was canonized.

The Princess and John Denver

In 1977 I went on a three-day hiking and camping excursion with John Denver. I knew John through EST, the popular self-help seminar of the day, as well as various charitable and environmental activities in which we were both involved.

I felt about John as much of the world saw and felt him—a tender, happy-go-lucky country boy with a sweet voice, long blond hair, oversized glasses, and happy songs that you couldn't help but hum once you had heard them a few times. His success was global and mammoth. At that time, he had sold one hundred million record albums, which put him in the Beatles and Presley universe.

I approached John and *Playboy Magazine* about my writing one of their lengthy Interviews with him. They accepted, as did John. He wouldn't permit any reporter access to his Aspen ranch, so instead suggested we go camping in Big Sur, in the Ventana Wilderness in northern California. He picked me up in San Francisco in his single-engine Cessna, for which he had JUST gotten his pilot's license. I was quite apprehensive about the flight, but game. John was silent and—thank you God—intensely focused as he piloted the small plane over the mountains. We—that is he, Ray his road manager, and I—flew to Monterey, then drove to Big Sur, past the luxurious Ventana Inn into the mountains.

Ray set up the tents, while I prayed for rain so that we could retreat to the inn. It quickly became clear that the entire trip was Nature Boy Meets Jewish Princess. I tripped over the tent moorings; Ray patiently reinstalled them. I was besieged by maddening killer gnats, John ignored them in favor of sighting distant hawks and deer on the hillsides. I tried to pretend that I was as cool as the two guys. I doubt they believed me, but they were kind and indulgent. I was a city girl, but also a reporter for a huge publication, about to write one of the near book-length interviews for which *Playboy* was celebrated.

There were many moments of true magic. The first night Ray grilled the lush steaks and we all drank the fine cabernet delivered up the mountain by the owner of the Ventana Inn. Then, we sat on the cliff together, John and I and his guitar, and a marijuana joint. The night was windless, balmy, and full mooned, the ocean glistening far below us. He began to play: "You fill up my senses, like a night in the forest", 'Annie's Song' written for his then-wife as his unique way of trying to salvage their faltering marriage. The song of course became one of his hallmarks. That night the mountains echoed with his pure tenor voice as he sang and played for more than an hour, nonstop, into the silence.

Timidly, I began to harmonize. I was a devoted fan and knew most of his songs. Over the next few days, we spent many hours sitting on this cliff. We sang almost everything he'd ever written, my vocal courage escalating as the time went on. "Rocky Mountain High" was one of my cheery favorites. Remember "Colorado Rocky Mountain High, I've seen it rainin' fire in the sky..." I didn't care if I ever did the interview, I was in heaven singing with John and his guitar. And the many joints that went along with the experience.

But of course, I did interview John extensively, uncovered the complex dark side of this world-renowned singer, composer, and humanitarian, his ego and fears, his easily triggered moods as well as his genuinely sweet, energetic self. He confessed: "my concerts are the most important thing in my life to me." They were the universe that made him feel truly alive. Given my own heady experience on the cliffs with John and his music, I could understand how his performances overshadowed everything else in his world.

He knew that the press had pulverized him for his "repellent narcissism" and "millionaire mediocrity", while in one year he sold more albums than any other artist in the world. When I questioned him about how he handled his bad reviews which appeared mostly in urban newspapers, he said, "the good ones I take as verbatim, as absolute gospel. The bad ones I dismiss." "Really?" I said, not believing him. "I know what was good and what was bad," he answered. "I know what I was trying to do and whether I succeeded or not. I've gotten out of the habit of reading reviews." Are you serious, I thought? I had never known a performer who didn't react strongly to reviews. John's complexity was not easily accessible to a journalist, even though we had known each other for a few years. I had spotted his vulnerability, his temper, his depression, several times in many situations.

One day we drove down to the beach, he climbed a wall of rocks while I took a delicious nap on the sand. It seemed an appropriate afternoon journey to me, in this scenario of Princess and Nature Boy. When I opened my eyes, he was making his way down the steep face of the rocks, carrying a bulging trash bag of beer cans and rubbish he'd collected at the top. "I'll never understand how people can crap up beautiful places like this," he snarled. Of course, I saw the committed naturalist in him, the country boy who would never leave the garbage out on the land.

That night he had offered to sing a few songs on the terrace of the Ventana Inn for the locals and tourists. The news spread throughout the Big Sur community. He began to sing at midnight and didn't stop until 2:30 in the morning. The audience of about seventy-five folks stayed until the end, gazing at the stars, drinking wine, and singing along. The magic was palpable, affecting everybody on the terrace. John was as content as I'd ever seen him.

The next afternoon we were sitting on the cliff taping the interview material when we spotted in the far distance a wall of smoke and fire heading towards Big Sur. Ray drove down the mountain to inform the inn staff. We packed up and spent the night in luscious comfort at the Ventana Inn. The next morning John flew us to Los Angeles in his Cessna. I finished the interview with him in LA, at his manager's home. It ran in *Playboy* a few months later and received much attention. John was not totally happy with how much of his vulnerability he had revealed and I had exposed.

I saw John several times over the next decade, and we'd always laugh about our camping adventure. He had a new wife and family and still lived in Aspen, recording and performing concerts around the world.

John died in 1997, at age fifty-three, piloting his small plane, in a terrible crash off the Monterey Peninsula—the same route that we had flown together twenty years before. By then, he had sold over 150 million albums.

Journey to Peru

A friend of mine, Roz K, a photographer in Berkeley, called and said, "How would you like to go to Peru, take psychedelics, and hang out with tropical shamans?" I answered, "When is the next plane?" And we were off.

The trip was organized and led by Alberto Villoldo, a teacher of all things mystical at San Francisco State. In his realm, he was a renowned young professor and seeker with far-out spiritual ideas and a growing following. He had led trips into the wilderness of Peru and had deep relationships with the shamans, healers, and the psychedelic drugs common to the area. *The New York Times* had labeled him "the Indiana Jones of the spirit world."

Life Magazine agreed to send me, pay my expenses

and that of my photographer friend, Roz, with the warning: "Don't get so stoned that you can't write." Roz and I had no idea what was in store but figured it would be a spectacular adventure.

We met the rest of our group—Alberto and 8 other Americans, mostly from the Berkeley/ San Francisco area—in Cusco, Peru, along with our first guide for the trip, Manuel Quispe, a medicine man and a native of the area, a man in his high sixties. Don Manuel was vibrant, stocky, about five foot eight, so muscular that I thought he could lift me over his head if he felt like it. He was a respected shaman whose work had created a substantial following all over Peru.

After exploring Cusco and environs, we learned how much of the population thrives on the leaves of the coca plants that dominate the area's agriculture—think "cocaine". We chewed tiny amounts of the leaves, getting somewhat stoned. We assumed the population of the farm areas was high most of the time. We also visited an oddly marked strip of bare land in the middle of the forest that the locals believe was created by the landing of UFOs. Then we set off for the sacred mountains of Machu Picchu.

In one of our group meetings, Don Manuel explained to us: "Machu Picchu was built by Pachacutek, the ninth Inca king, who ruled an empire the size of the United States. The name means 'old peak.' It's the most mystical site in Peru." It's a mountainous Andes area, more than 7000 feet above sea level, built around the year 1400. Machu Picchu consists of more than 150 ancient stone buildings ranging from baths and houses to temples, and 100 separate flights of stairs carved from stones. Although many of the stones weighed more than fifty pounds each, the legend says they were carried up the mountain by hundreds of men pushing these enormous rocks up the steep slopes. All the structures were built so that the rocks fit perfectly together, with no mortar, so that not even a knife blade can fit between them. And this was 700 years ago...

Due to its location high in the mountains, every day until roughly midday, a blanket of mist covers Machu Picchu. This creates the feeling of floating amongst the clouds. However, legend has it that at night, spirits rise from the ground and try to take people away. To protect against this, most porters to this day will sleep with a mirror beneath them to defy the spirits. I never understood how this is supposed to work.

This mountain community was rooted in the idea of healing and the secret spirit world. The mythical ancient potion, ayahuasca, was used by shamans and medicine men to experience the realm beyond this life.

Nowadays Machu Picchu is overrun with tourists, having been declared one of the New Seven Wonders of the World in 2007. But when my small group, led by Alberto and Don Manuel journeyed there decades ago, it was still almost empty, with only one funky hotel and no sense of tourism.

Our plan was to stay just for the day and then take the train down the mountain. It was dramatic, beautiful, but eerie and foggy, with a piercing cold. We hiked, climbed up and down many of the stairs, and did strange rituals led by our two guides, whose purpose was for us to experience the ancient practices, the energies, and a sense of this sacred place. I sat on the edge of a cliff for an hour, alone, staring into another cliff, in a unique mental state such that I imagined I could see humans inside the cliff. We had taken a small bit of ayahuasca during the day, but this part of the expedition was not meant to be experienced while stoned.

None of us wanted to leave in the afternoon, we pleaded with our guides to stay overnight. But there was no room at the small inn, so Alberto concocted another way to sleep. He found a cave where the llamas went to keep warm and dry and arranged a sleeping situation for us ten people. We laid on top of one another, five on the bottom, another five on top of them. Of course, we had no blankets, only our own heavy jackets and each other for warmth. What we did have was our sense of adventure and the rank smell of the llamas, who thank heaven chose not to visit their cave that night. If I slept at all, it was not more than a few moments here and there, and only from the exhaustion of the day and the need not to think about the food that we didn't have.

A few days later, we all journeyed to Lima and then up the coast to Trujillo, the home of an active and large tribe of medicine men and women healers. Most of us rented cars, so we could have a few days to explore the coast. Roz and I and three guys from our group set out, planning to find a motel to spend the night. But, as darkness came and we didn't pass any place to stay, we knew we'd have to sleep on the beach. The night was tropical, moonless, and when we were too tired to continue, we found a dark beach and crashed on the sand. Well, there was an odd, unpleasant odor, but we couldn't see anything and were able to sleep for a few hours until dawn. When we woke at sunrise and looked to the left, we saw we had camped on the edge of a large garbage dump. Hence the smell. We all stunk. Roz the photographer said: "I'm going to take a zillion pictures of this place because nobody will believe this!"

Then Trujillo: a city near the beach, whose main industries are shoes and white asparagus. Besides several large cathedrals and a sizable Catholic population, there was a fascinating marketplace where we spent much time over the three days that we were there. Our guide for this part of the journey was Eduardo Calderon, a very tall and stocky man who trained with sorcerers in his youth before he walked the path of becoming a shaman healer. He was likable, interesting, and calm. He introduced us to a much bigger amount of ayahuasca than we had yet experienced. He reminded us that it is a sacred plant to the people of the upper Amazon, who believe they can journey to the domains beyond death when they ingest it.

A woman had joined our group for this portion of the trip. She had been blinded in an auto accident a few years before and in connecting with Alberto in Berkeley, he told her that the shamans in Trujillo might be able to help her regain her sight. Barbara was about thirty, self-contained, and able to maneuver cleverly on her own.

That night, Alberto and Eduardo took us to the beach and fed us ayahuasca. It was a profound experience for me of communing with my father who had passed, and having a general emotional healing that to this day is impossible to describe. After that night, Barbara began to see again, hazy sights, never clear. It lasted two days, then she lost it. I wanted to say something to her, as we all did, but we didn't know what to say.

Trujillo had a typical thriving outdoor market, much of which consisted of medicine people selling their spiritual wares and proffering wisdom. I stopped to see the goods of a woman with piercing brown eyes, who in perfect English said to me: "Your mother is a harsh woman. You must make distance between you." She was correct. She gave my friend Roz insights about her ex-husband that were shocking in their accuracy.

This was near the end of our Peruvian adventure. We returned to Lima, stayed in a hotel with serious beds and thick steaks, and I spent the trip home and for many months afterward recalling the lifetime's worth of the peculiar, deep, and ecstatic experiences. I'll never forget staring into the cliff in Machu Picchu and observing the old souls living there. I never took ayahuasca again.

Yes, Drugs

I would never consider myself a drug person. Or a person who, like some of my friends, is constantly searching for the latest high. I get my thrills, these years, from a vodka and tonic with a lot of fresh lime juice.

But I'm a child of the '60s, of the drugs/sex/ rock & roll era, which is another way of saying that dope in various forms is neither alien nor frightening nor overwhelmingly thrilling to me. And when I talk of dope, I don't mean heroin, opiates, anything injectable or life-threatening. Although I suppose an argument could be made that too many vodka and tonics could kill you. But you know what I mean.

The first time I smoked marijuana—perhaps later to be referred to as grass, pot, or weed—was with

my pal Jerry in my apartment in Greenwich Village.
He brought over a joint, yes it was illegal then, so of
course doubly exciting. He taught me how to inhale,
a different process than my previous days of cigarette
smoking, and after two puffs I was catapulted to a
strange new land. What I remember most after all
these decades was Jerry and I giggling, laughing in
hysterics, and feeling that every thought and word
that came out of our mouths was the funniest thing
anybody had ever said or heard. It was such a life-
altering experience I'm surprised I didn't become a
weed addict on the spot. I didn't find God, Nirvana,
or the true meaning of life that night, I only laughed
with unspeakable silliness for many hours.

I did smoke grass for many years after that, sometimes regularly and sometimes sporadically, depending on whom I was with. I don't think I ever smoked
it alone; it was always a social activity for me.

The drug I remember having the most interesting effect on me was Ecstasy and I have to brag—if
bragging is the correct verb here—that I was one of
the first people to take it in L.A. Soon after I married
Tom, we were going out to the desert, to a very cool
resort called Two Bunch Palms, for a weekend with
another couple, close friends. We wanted to bring
some pot with us to smoke in the luxurious hot tub,
or while having massages or strolling in the desert.

Another friend, a book publisher in LA, had just
acquired a bit of this new drug, Ecstasy, from Tim-
othy Leary, who was well-known in town for his

cutting-edge relationship with various mind-altering substances. Our friend Jeremy, while giving us a small supply for the four of us, told us this was a drug becoming known for its ability to create love, generate commitment, and—yes—ecstasy between a couple. In fact, Leary had just married his long-term girlfriend after a few small doses of the drug.

The four of us took it, had the experiences that were forecast as well as several others. There was a huge, gnarled oak tree outside of Tom's and my cabin and one afternoon we four spent about two hours sitting silently in front of it, just staring at it while it seemed to come alive for us. "Look at that branch," Tom gurgled. "It looks just like our dog." Indeed it did. "I never have to go anywhere else but this tree," exclaimed our friend Donna. These expressions were so logical and natural to us. Of course.

Ecstasy seemed to inspire a deep level of soul-gazing and introspection in me for about a year, as well as loving times with my mate. Once I took it with these same two friends while Tom was out of town. I planted my naked self on the floor in front of a wall-to-wall mirror in my office. For several hours I stared at every pore, freckle, wrinkle, and deep into my own green eyes. I was fascinated by myself, much less critical than my normal journeys into my physical self. In these current years, Ecstasy of course has become a street drug, available everywhere but your local 7-11 and much less pristine. I haven't been interested in it for many years.

Then there was the fabulous group mushroom trip. Marilyn Ferguson was a New Age guru who wrote a best-selling book called *The Aquarian Conspiracy*. She surrounded herself with hip folks who followed her lead on all matters of mind expansion and saving the planet. Her boyfriend Ray was an optometrist who always had his parrot on his left shoulder, frequently wiping up the bird's shit.

Marilyn had a large party one Sunday afternoon where she provided psychedelic mushrooms for the whole gang. I'd never had them before. They inspired all the guests to fall in love with one another. A guy whom I'd known slightly from other New Age events sidled up to me, saying, "your eyes look like they could end war forever." I was so stoned I didn't realize what a dumb remark it was until the next day.

I suppose if this was a slightly different kind of group it would have wound up in a mass orgy, but in this gathering of largely spiritual 1980's folk, the outpouring was of optimism, the dedication to ending hunger on the planet, and the commitment to Marilyn's buckets of divine vegetarian pasta salad.

It wasn't just a decades-long series of magical moments. There were some bum trips as well, which you would expect, as I learned over time. Once, about five years ago, Tom and I were on a plane from LA to Paris. We had given up smoking anything by then as we were concerned about our aging lungs and there were so many substitutes easily available. He had brought some edible gummies with him, little candies to chew. I ate one or two and soon freaked out, had the sort of deep panic attack that I'd never had before. Talking to myself about how this was only a drug trip, not a real-life experience, and other positive bromides was unconvincing. I was in full terror mode. I walked up and down the aisles, certain we were about to crash until Tom thought to give me an Ambien sleeping pill. Soon the crisis was over, and I slept the rest of the way to Paris. My life with gummies was finished, it only took one bad adventure. I also never take anything on planes anymore.

This piece could be an encyclopedia of drug advances in this hip day of legalization. There are names like Indica and Sativa and initials—CBD and THC—for pain, deep relaxation, sleep, joyous awakening in the morning. My actor friend takes psychedelic mushrooms before her auditions, and no longer experiences the anxiety she always did. My neighborhood has giant billboards advertising free dope delivery; a nearby boulevard has a huge store called Med Men, with lines down the street at all hours.

The more things change *dotdotdot*. Humans still want to get stoned, for two hundred reasons. Peruvian Indians take ayahuasca for healing, for seeing into life after this one. I take very little of anything these recent years and usually just for sleep. My mushrooms take the form of creamy risotto. My vodka and tonic does the trick. I'm no longer cool.

Climate and Change

I thought we were going to change the world and help end the climate crisis. Tom and I spent a year of our lives working on this noble project, under the strange and ultimately fruitless direction of one of the most complex humans I've ever known, Jordan McBain.

It started in Cleveland. We went to a three-day conference, sponsored by an institute at Case Western University to talk about the role of business in benefitting the planet. This was really Tom's universe; I went just for fun and to see several good friends from around the country who were attending.

At the beginning of every morning's session and at various times during the day, a handsome, smooth-haired classical violinist of about forty-five years old, named Jordan McBain, inspired us by playing Bach for the group. He was intense, charismatic, a somewhat '60s hippie in a room of sports-jacketed business consultants, which made him unique and quite popular. I adored him as soon as he played one of Bach's violin sonatas.

Several of us had dinner one night and Jordan told us of his life's passion, a project he had created in his hometown of Aspen Colorado. It was named One Planet and his vision was thrilling: There was going to be a live global event where large international companies would show their public commitment to working on climate change. This would be followed by a giant streamed concert, taking place all over the world. There would be appearances by the Dalai Lama and perhaps the Pope, both of whom Jordan knew. It was going to happen within two years. I'm simplifying the event, but this was the basic outline.

Over lavish French desserts, all twelve people at the table exclaimed "WE'RE IN". That was the beginning of a year Tom and I spent in several spots in America and France following Jordan and his violin, briefly directing the whole project, and finally experiencing some of the saddest disappointments of my adult years.

In early December we held a three-day meeting at our home in Los Angeles. Eighteen colleagues from all over the country attended, along with Jordan of course. Every morning we began the day with bagels, a violin solo, and a meditation about altering the growing climate crisis and manifesting Jordan's dream. We then planned, wrote notes on a flipchart, ate pizza, and dreamed big. We assigned aspects of the project to various people. We brainstormed locations for the concert and corporate conference, created a preliminary budget, explored ways to get companies to participate. The joy of the three days was Jordan articulating more and more details of his huge vision.

Over the next few months, Tom and I, assigned to creating publicity and enlisting our contacts in the entertainment business, moved ahead with One Planet. Jordan, meanwhile, was creating some amazing relationships. He was playing concerts around the world and had this ability to chat up powerful guys—and they all seemed to be "guys"—on planes and enroll them in helping him. That was his uncanny charisma. On one flight he sat next to a Frenchman named Andre Bal who owned an 18th century estate called Chateau St. Pierre, one hour west of Paris, which he loaned to dance companies, acting troupes, and corporations for retreats. By the time the flight was over Andre had offered the chateau to Jordan to use for a meeting the following summer.

Another flight had Jordan sitting next to the CEO of a software company from Silicon Valley who became optimistic about the project and was a potential source of financing for us. Tom offered to accompany Jordan up north to this man's office for a serious business conversation about sponsorship.

Jordan refused, insisting it was too soon and he would approach him personally, not in his office. He was adamant, and this was the first time we saw the defensive, childlike quality in Jordan that would eventually drive us nuts. The software exec disappeared after a short time without any of the rest of us making a connection. We were frustrated, but somehow not surprised. Tom believed that he should take over One Planet to run it like a real business. Jordan seemed relieved. He was the genius, the source of the vision, but not the businessman.

Not much happened over the spring of that year. More people met Jordan and became captivated, a few more meetings. We came up again and again with Jordan's resistance, he blocked our taking action and blamed it on his board in Aspen.

Then in June, twenty-two of us from all over the globe traveled to Chateau St. Pierre. Andre wasn't kidding about loaning Jordan his huge property with hundreds of acres close to Paris. Andre would stay there and attend the meeting. He had bedrooms and baths for the whole group; these were in some need of repair but nonetheless, it was a rare experience to be housed in an 18th-century chateau. I'm sure for many of the group this journey was an excuse to go to Paris and to visit this spectacular historic property. But still, everybody there was committed to the project. Climate change was in the headlines, the crisis was getting more frightening every week, and each of us wanted to do something huge and noteworthy. An impressive, powerful group of folks from all over the world descended on St. Pierre, all of whom were there because of Jordan's ability to entice them.

I now believe that the more real One Planet became, the more frightened Jordan became, and the more difficult it was for him to anchor himself in reality. He played the violin a lot at the chateau, frequently under the trees where we all walked on breaks from meetings, when Jordan would talk on and on about what a world-changing event this would be. Speaking with the other participants—philanthropists, climate activists, and scientists—was the liveliest part of the meeting. That and the extravagant dinners with which Andre regaled us within his giant antique-filled dining room. At one such dinner, an opera singer whom Andre had brought out from Paris performed, accompanied by a piano... and Jordan's violin, of course. The amazing food was also imported from Paris.

Jordan had mailed to everybody ahead of time that we could expect a very experienced meeting facilitator who worked at Google. We discovered this young fellow, Jeffrey, was intimidated by the guest list and was terrible at what he was supposed to be doing, namely organizing the meeting, and keeping it on track. Instead, he wandered around the room carrying a flipchart, looking vague and distant. Everything was getting peculiar and then Jordan and Andre disappeared for hours. We later discovered that they had a falling out and Andre's participation in the future project was problematic. By the end of the meeting, even after all he had contributed, Andre was finished.

And everybody else became disillusioned. Nothing had happened that was concrete or substantive. We had lost our faith in Jordan. Tom and I bowed out of One Planet. He never spoke to us again.

Two years later, after the promised event had not yet happened, a wealthy technology magnate took over One Planet and fired Jordan. Last year it disappeared, getting absorbed into a climate change organization with a very different journey.

I still feel the pangs of disappointment that the grand dream never became real. And I have no idea what happened to the genius violinist.

Into Africa

Someone said you can't take a bad photo in Africa. That's possibly true, and you also can't tell a dreary anecdote that involves animals in the wild.

I fell in love with Kenya on my first trip, before I knew Tom, as a journalist. It was the animals on the plains that stirred my soul, a place where I was always unnecessary, irrelevant, just an observer of ancient beauty and order. I always have felt the presence of something I might call God while in the wilds of Africa.

Tom and I have made eight trips to Eastern and Southern Africa on safari. That includes six countries and dozens of stories. On our first trip together, to Kenya and Tanzania, the second day there included one of our most heart-stopping escapades.

KENYA: There were six of us on this trip, two

good friends, David and Karen, and a honeymoon couple we had just met. We were a good-natured and adventurous troupe. On our first night of camping in the Masai Mara, a vast Kenya game reserve, we were well protected and cared for by the staff of ten. At about 2:00 in the morning, we were awakened in our tents by two gunshots in the distance. Our guide bolted into the campsite and shouted to us to dress immediately.

Guns are a rare sight in the game parks, although the guides carry them, well-hidden for the rare emergencies. The sound of gunshots was one I'd never heard before that night. Tom and I tossed on some clothes in the freezing dark tent and bolted to our jeep. Some considerate helpmate handed us paper cups of hot tea and a few biscuits to take on the ride. Off we all went, trailing the gunshots. I was worked up by the ominous adventure of it all, but had no idea what it all meant or what we would find.

What happened next: our driver-guide, an experienced and unruffled professional, raced toward where we had heard the gunshots. On his walkie-talkie device, he got the entire story. Two game wardens on patrol during the night saw lion tracks moving in the direction of where they knew a white rhinoceros and her baby lived. They fired warning shots to scare the lion off but hadn't seen him. Those were the two shots that had awakened us in the camp.

Northern white rhinos are a rare, endangered breed in Africa—today, there are only two remaining in the world, they are kept in a conservancy in Kenya, protected by round-the-clock armed guards. At that time there were more, but they were being poached for their horns, which were considered a valuable commodity, particularly in Asia.

As we scrambled across the plains, any remnants of sleep left me. We drove frantically, we all became agitated, as we didn't know what we would find, and imagined the worst scenario—that the lion had murdered one of the rhinos. Our guide was in constant touch with the game wardens who had seen the lion tracks stalking the baby. We drove for a few hours, joining the hunt for the baby, after spotting the mother in a clearing, looking forlorn. At least I interpreted her enormous face as forlorn.

It was now about 5:00 in the morning, getting light. Finally, we got word that the game warden had killed the lion, after we heard the third gunshot. We were all relieved, even without any information about the baby's welfare. After an hour of circling the area, the game wardens reported that the two rhinos were reunited, back in their home area, grazing. Finally, I relaxed. I had had a tortured time imagining a huge lion tearing apart a rare baby rhino.

After another hour of driving on bumpy dirt roads, we came to a Maasai village and spotted the huge lion carcass hanging, the hide skinned, the head still on. The tribe was surrounding the lion's remains, anticipating their future meal. We spent some time—taking pictures of course—communicating as best we could with the welcoming natives. We understood the lion would be dinner that night. I thought, "everybody has to survive, it's the basic rule." The next day the story of the chase and rescue was on the front page of the Nairobi newspaper.

For me, it was always difficult and confusing watching a kill in the wild. These events are what my human mind projects as brutal, cruel, ugly. I've had to work my mind around "survival of the fittest" and "law of the jungle" notions in order not to be sickened by the sight. I've had to remind myself that everybody must eat and I'm in the wilds of Africa, not near a supermarket. Usually, my self-talk works; if not, I just turn away.

After a few days of animal watching in the Maasai Mara game reserve, we drove back to Nairobi. We had dinner at the most popular restaurant in town, appropriately called "Carnivore". It's where all tourists were shepherded at least once as they passed through town. The name is perfect. The buffet menu consisted of, in addition to every known concoction of beef, lamb, and pork, such delicacies as giraffe, crocodile, and ox balls—all farm-raised they said, nothing gleaned from the wild. "Oh my God," I groaned while looking at a giant vat of crocodile meat, "where's the salmon?" No fish at the Carnivore. Tom tasted everything—zebra, gazelle, wildebeest. I stuck with chicken wings and steak. I could have been back in LA.

ZIMBABWE: On still another trip, we visited Victoria Falls. It straddles the countries of Zambia and

Zimbabwe and is one of the seven natural wonders of the world. We flew over the Falls in a helicopter, hiked around the Falls in the rainforest, took a million pictures, and cruised on the Zambezi River. We went back to the Falls at night when there is an unbelievable rainbow glowing in the dark. "Can we live here?" I begged Tom. He paid no attention since I always ask that when we come upon a spectacular place anywhere in the world. I was in heaven, as I always am in the presence of breathtaking beauty. Not a world of animals here, but the overwhelming Victoria Falls compensated.

One night our hotel sent us to Boma, another restaurant created for wide-eyed tourists. They had a gigantic buffet like Carnivore in Nairobi, but with crocodile ravioli, something called mopane worms (I never even looked), and warthog. All the accouterments of over-the-top touristic entertaining. An unrelenting drum and dance show, a sarong placed on each of the female guests as we entered the premises, dots painted on our cheeks to signify the beauty of African women, men painted with stripes for the warrior look of the males. Tom looked absurd in his khaki pants and green t-shirt, his face covered with white stripes.

There was also a bombardment of enforced dancing and exuberance. But I let go of my western cynicism and got into it, after all this was Zimbabwe, a once-in-a-lifetime experience. Not a time to be sophisticated Americans. I ate roasted lamb, Tom and our friends tasted all the eccentricities. I did keep thinking that maybe his warthog was the one hanging out by our hotel room that morning. I couldn't even look at it.

TANZANIA: In the summer of 2018, we went to Tanzania with a small group of friends for two weeks. We traveled with Anglebert Pantaleo in his Toyota Land Cruiser. Because of the pervasive dryness resulting from the climate crisis in the area, the dirt roads were dusty and quite bumpy; everybody ended the trip with some kind of injury. I did something permanent to a joint in my right shoulder. But it was a beautiful journey of wild animal sightings.

The most mind-bending excursion was to the Mara River where a gathering of thousands, yes truly, thousands of wildebeests, huddled by the shore and up on the hills, unmoving. Anglebert parked our vehicle on the opposite side of the river from the animals, hidden behind trees as he claimed the animals would scurry out of view if they saw us. He warned us we could expect to be stationary for perhaps several hours while the wildebeests did nothing, didn't move at all. After taking two dozen photos of the placid hoards, I settled back and read several chapters of a mystery novel on my iPad.

Suddenly, a few hours later, after seeing nothing happening but these black creatures gathering on the river beach and on the hills, one single wildebeest leaped forward, bolted across the river and the thousands of others bolted after him. The migration continued for about forty-five minutes as every one of the wildebeests galloped down from the hills and headed across the river in a swell of strong current and noise. Anglebert, our savvy guide had no reasonable explanation for why the giant horde followed the "leader". He also told us that after a few hours on the other side, they would repeat the sequence and head back. The next day would be the same opera. It was the strangest, most baffling occurrence I had ever seen in Africa.

All of these unpredictable, fantastic adventures changed me, my relationship to animals, and to the complex drama of life. I've never felt that I was finished with Africa, that I've seen and done it all. After nine adventures into the African wild, I always long to go back and back. And back.

The Last Supper

I loathe camping. Any sleeping situation that doesn't include a private bathroom a few steps from my bed is, to my sensibility, torture. In some of the roughest circumstances in my life, the tent was tiny (I'm also claustrophobic), and the alleged firm bed was surely constructed for a solitary confinement cell at Attica Prison.

Nonetheless, there I was with Tom and our close friends Richard and Maryanne, camping for four days in the Ngorongoro Crater in Tanzania in primitive tents. It was decided by the guides for this exquisite three-week jaunt through East Africa that the best way to experience the astounding crater, instead of staying at the only hotel on the rim, was to camp right inside the crater, to be close to the animals roaming the area. And to cook our own food, instead of dining at a mere hotel restaurant which was removed from the sounds and smells that coursed through the land far below. At the time, this choice made perfect sense to us.

A bit of background: The Ngorongoro Crater is vast, fourteen miles wide, the distance from Hollywood to Santa Monica, formed when a huge volcano erupted and collapsed on itself. It is one of the seven natural wonders of Africa, home to over 30,000 animals—the densest collection of wildlife on the entire continent—with the world's largest lion population. While giraffes are common throughout all the wildlife regions in the country, there are none in the crater as their long skinny legs could not make it down the steep slopes from the rim.

We drove into the crater in some form of large land rover, a rough and daunting excursion. En route, we passed a dozen Maasai tribesmen herding their cattle and sheep which, for some bizarre reason, live peacefully with the lions and leopards that stalk the area, among the most fertile grazing grounds in Africa. The Maasai are, in general, a very tall and thin tribe. They were all wearing muted colored shawls and short pants, which I thought was odd, considering where they walk in the forest and jungle.

Our driver stopped next to one Maasai farmer, had a spirited conversation, which of course we didn't understand, but soon he returned carrying an adorable small lamb which he placed in the luggage portion in the back of our vehicle. I had a bad feeling about this transaction. The lamb was bleating unhappily, and so was I.

They pulled the vehicle into the campsite, where the trip's Sherpas were setting up our minuscule tents. The lamb was tied up in the section where the Sherpas slept, and we were told he would be our dinner the following night. I gasped, for some reason not having fully considered the obvious implications of the lamb purchase.

I wanted to give him a name. "What about Baaa-Baaa?" I begged. Tom warned me: "Do not name him, you will only become attached and suffer." I planned the lamb's escape. I would cut him loose while everybody was sleeping, and he would return home to his flock. The story would end well.

When I told Tom and our friends that I was going to release him, Richard, a scientist and scholar, said, "Are you nuts? He'll be food for a lion in four minutes. It's better we kill him humanely and enjoy eating him." Unfortunately, this made sense, the lamb was doomed, no matter what we did. So I relented but didn't sleep well that night. I knew animals being killed and eaten was one of the primary laws of the wild, and I was far from being a vegan, but I was having a terrible time with this slaughter. BaaaBaaa was so cute.

The next day we toured the amazing crater, spotting lions, buffalo, hyenas, monkeys, and predators of every sort. We saw a leopard stalking a wildebeest, which is an astounding sight, another reminder of the ineffable rules of the natural world. I had no desire to try to save the wildebeest, as I did the lamb. When we got back to the campsite, after a glorious sunset, they had already killed and seasoned the lamb and had started the fire. By then I'd worked my head around the permission to kill and eat meat, guaranteed by my beef-centric upbringing and my local supermarket. I said a silent blessing over him. Dinner that night around the campfire, I was forced to admit, was sublime, the best rack of lamb I've ever tasted.

But another adventure was in store, when Tom woke up in the middle of the night, shrieking. Fire ants had invaded our tent and his shoes and pajamas were covered with the tiny critters. He ran outside, one of the staff came with some ant killer and apologized for not having dug a trench around the tents to prevent the crossing of the ants into our sleeping area.

Our friends next door had the same disgusting problem. Everyone was invaded by ants—but me. They ignored me. Tom said he knew there was a God that night when the ants left me alone. "They must have known how much you hate camping," he said.

The next day was another remarkable adventure in the crater with more animals than I'd ever seen gathered in one area in Africa. "I could live here," I declared to everyone, not meaning in the tent with the bugs, of course. Tom rolled his eyes.

That night we and our friends abandoned the campsite, got a ride up to the rim, and stayed overnight at the only hotel. It was sparse and primitive, but had real beds, and a tiny bathroom with a real shower. I couldn't hear animals roaring or smell the trees or feel the wind that night, but I was in heaven.

Nine Summers

I remember nine glorious summers of my life. They took place in a tiny town in the Bernese Oberland area of the Swiss Alps, between Interlaken and Lucerne. Our dear pals, Sherry and Bill, discovered this remote village, named Reuti, on an earlier trip, fell in love with its breathtaking views of the mountains, its incredible hiking (some easy, some arduous), and its opulent sausages. They urged us to join them for two weeks the following summer. After our first excursion, we knew we would go back and back and back. And so we did, for a few weeks every summer for nine years.

Everything about Reuti was magical: It had few tourists, and they were serious hikers; it had no t-shirt shops or discos. There was a chairlift that went down the mountain to Meiringen, the local town that had an actual supermarket with wonderful cheeses and boundless fresh fruit. We rode down there every few days to stack up for meals to cook. Reuti was so small, quiet, and hidden that when we were in Meiringen it felt like "the big city", and rather overwhelmed us. In fact, Meiringen is where Sherlock Holmes was (fictionally) killed by being pushed over Reichenbach Falls. There is a statue of Sherlock in the town square. Every tourist takes photos next to the Holmes statue. We took several while hiking next to the Falls.

Sometimes it would be just the four of us, sometimes younger family members joined us and would go off on their more challenging hikes each morning. Often additional friends came to Reuti and were astounded by the Alpine magnificence surrounding us.

Every summer was unique, although we had our favorite hikes which we repeated year after year. We always walked around a lake and stopped at the same restaurant for a seafood lunch. We hiked on a trail that had dozens of wood sculptures crafted by local artists. We walked with the cows and howled at their eyelashes. We took a lift to the wondrous expanse at the top of our local mountain, stopped for rich Swiss coffee, and hiked back down into town for an afternoon nap. As many times as we repeated our best-loved walks, they never felt the same, always new, deeper, and richer, as the memories built up and were more satisfying with each trip.

Reuti had a population of just a few hundred, one general store, a few simple outdoor restaurants, one hotel, and a dozen rental homes. Our yearly home was made of dark oak, was nothing fancy but had beautiful views of the mountains, flowers all around its borders, and soft feather quilts to sink our exhausted bodies underneath at night.

Most important, it had a small bus stop and a chairlift so we could leave town every morning for our daily adventures at precisely 9:00—Swiss transportation is NEVER late. One morning the bus was fifteen minutes late and we speculated that this was the end of life as we'd known it. It had never happened before or ever again.

We hiked all over the Bernese area, up and down green hills and mountains, around blue lakes, by waterfalls, into postcard lovely towns. We ate cheese-filled lunches on hilltop terraces. We all got deeply tan. Late in the afternoon we took the bus back into Reuti, settled down for a few beers on the terrace of the local pizza pub, watching the sunset fall over the mountains. Evening was for barbecuing, lots of wine, raucous laughing, and poker. We felt blessed every day.

On the rare day when it was drizzling or cloudy, we took the train along Lake Lucerne into the city, visited the famous modern art museum with its Picassos and Klees. We strolled along the cobblestone streets with medieval houses, shopped at the open-air flea markets, ate lunch at the Burgerstube or some other classic Swiss haunt. As charming as this city life was, we couldn't wait to get back to our remote village, our magical mountains, and quiet times together.

Sherry and Bill are both gone, our hiking bodies are more vulnerable, and those nine summers are exquisite memories that still fill us with gratitude whenever we bring them out.

UFO Encounters

In 1977, I was collaborating with Steven Spielberg on a book about the making of his epic movie *Close Encounters of the Third Kind*, which was to be released about a month from then. Steven was a lifelong believer in the UFO phenomenon and was obsessed with the possibility of encountering one. I had had several recent interactions in the UFO world, which is how he came to me and invited me to write the book with him.

We spent much of every day and all evening, for many weeks, working on the book, talking, and writing. He was still shooting last-minute tiny scenes for the movie, some not more than forty-five seconds long, that would haunt him during sleepless nights. But one night, at his insistence, we stopped writing at about 8:00. He had a fierce longing which he felt compelled to follow. He yearned for a close encounter of ANY kind. (The "third kind" means a meeting with an actual alien being.) He summoned his driver, who picked us up and drove us out into the desert, on the freeway from Los Angeles towards Palm Springs. We settled on an unoccupied stretch of land and walked into the dark desert. We then put blankets on the earth and lay staring at the sky. I was confused, had a jumbled idea of what we were really doing there, until he explained: "I think this is the night I'm going to see a UFO. I can just feel it. I deserve it, don't you think?" I agreed, if there is such a thing as deserving a UFO sighting, Steven should have it. Me, probably not so much.

I believe in the existence of UFOs. I have no doubt that there are alien beings in space, hovering about in our unfathomable universe in their strange interplanetary vehicles. Why not? It makes perfect sense to me. I know certainly that they are being studied by our secret government groups, as well as reputed scientists and anybody who cares, like the five million hobbyist buffs and the few hundred UFO organizations throughout America. I've had several experiences over a few decades which—although they were not direct and only fourth-hand—nonetheless made me become a true believer.

Steven Spielberg, at age sixteen, wrote, directed, and edited a 2½-hour film called *Firelight*, the subject of which was an invasion from space monsters against the National Guard. *Close Encounters* was brewing inside him since childhood. He told me that "growing up thinking about UFOs was like growing up with Presley and the Beatles and Howdy Doody."

One of his most heartfelt memories was as a boy having missed his Boy Scout troop outing when, at midnight in the Arizona desert, they all saw what they believed was a true UFO, he said, a "blood-red orb rising up behind some sagebrush, shooting off into space." He felt heartbroken at being left out. Then while on location in Alabama for *Close Encounters* he saw his first UFO, one of the most thrilling moments of his life. "When I found out later that it was only an Echo satellite I was as depressed as I've ever been."

Usually, there isn't much conversation in the mainstream media about UFOs. It's too weird and has nothing to do with Donald Trump. But during 2021 the talk surfaced into the public again through an uptick in odd sightings, largely over military bases. The Senate Intelligence Committee has been looking at it and released a report at the end of June that was totally inconclusive about what these objects are. But the report hinted that they don't believe the 144 known sightings in recent years are extraterrestrial but rather "advanced technologies that are in our restricted airspace almost on a nightly basis." They also claimed many of these objects could be birds, drones, or balloons. Many people question the truth of this report, of course.

I became fascinated by the subject back in 1976. I

was asked, by a magazine of which I was a Contributing Editor, to attend a conference in Acapulco, with the solemn title of The First International Congress of Unidentified Flying Objects. It had a collection of 1,500 guests, twenty-seven panelists from eleven countries, all members of the subterranean cult of UFOlogists. The range of fascinated citizens was amazing. Many were highly respected astronomers, mathematicians, physicists, clergymen, social scientists but there were also hundreds of folks with advanced degrees in nuttyometry. At least 200 have had or believe they've had a common experience of a UFO interaction that has altered their lives. Me, I was just a skeptical journalist who thrived on strange adventures.

The conference was as truly bizarre as one would imagine, with dozens of personal reports of UFO sightings, called "cases". Some were already reported in the underground libraries of more than 100 books (my favorite title was *God Drives a Flying Saucer*). Other reports came from thriving groups like the Ground Saucer Watch out of Phoenix. Personal dissension ran amok as experts and true believers argued over what this reality could all be.

I became exhilarated by the reams of stories and tall tales that ran through the conference, personal chats on the floor, and then at the bars and cafes where we spent our off-hours, sometimes until the middle of the night. The entire conversation was about the phenomenon of personal interactions, the "close encounters of the third kind." (The first two kinds were CE 1, for short, which means sighting a UFO; CE 2 meaning changes in the surroundings, like radioactive remains). CE 3 reports are the most impossible to verify, fearsome, and the most gripping.

At one extreme of attendees were the "nuts and bolts" guys, the scientists from many fields who insist UFOs are extraterrestrial in origin, with the purpose of surveillance of the planet and examination of our human bodies. The other extreme were guys who were "contactees", who claim to have had a close experience with space visitors. Religious components—the appearance of a savior and miraculous happenings—lie at the root of contacteeism. Neither group, the scientists or the CE 3 people, had tolerance for or interest in the other. I didn't know what to make of either set: As my knowledge expanded a bit at a time, the pure science world seemed limited, and the contactees seemed to my dizzy brain like total fruitcakes.

But the issue had begun to haunt me. One panelist, the only one who did not perceive the UFO as benign, was terrified of an intergalactic space war—a sentiment once actually spouted by General Douglas MacArthur. Another scientist, who showed promise of being the only voice of sobriety and sanity in these proceedings began his talk with: "An expert has studied UFOs long enough to realize he is utterly ignorant. The UFO is the outstanding strange dilemma of our age. We don't know WHAT they are."

This was from Dr. Allen Hynek, chairman of the Northwestern University Department of Astronomy.

The question that haunted the conference, and me, is an obvious and timeless one: In this universe of billions of galaxies, why would we assume we're the only creatures around? I asked myself this many times during the four days of the conference and long afterward. From time to time, I am still asking it, all these decades later.

After I came home I wrote a cover story for New West Magazine called "Are They Here?" I also began work, with a writer friend, on a children's book called *UFO Encounters*, and was soon approached by Steven Spielberg to write with him. I relished the opportunity. So, there we were a few months later, out in the desert at midnight searching for extraterrestrial spacecraft and little green men.

I thought we both were worthy of a sighting, he for all his years of obsession, me for my few months of studying, thinking, writing, reading, and, yes, obsessing. We lay there without speaking for an hour, saw nothing but a clear, gorgeous, limitless star-filled sky which was and is mysterious and infinite. I live on a beach, where stars and a few planets are plentiful, and I gaze longingly at the sky. Years after that night with Steven in the desert, I'm still looking. And hoping.

Theatre Life

From Journalism
To Theatre

For twenty years I was a journalist, living in both New York and Los Angeles. I was successful, I had a book on the bestseller list, another was sold to the movies. I traveled to Africa, India, Peru, and all over America to write articles and research my books. I wrote for almost every major magazine in America. I covered Tricia Nixon's wedding at the White House and wrote long interviews for *Playboy*. It was a fascinating and gratifying life.

One day I simply decided I never wanted to write again. It happened while I was writing a book with my husband, Tom, on the subject of Good Marriage. We had been married for about five minutes when we got the contract from Random House. Neither of us had any idea what it took to make a good or even a terrible marriage, and we spent the next year jaunting around the country interviewing couples who had been married twenty years or more. They claimed to know something about the secrets to having a successful marriage.

When it was time to write the book, the chore fell to me as the writer in this marriage. Tom, who was a respected and successful corporate consultant, went off to see clients every day, or traveled monthly to Chicago for four days to visit local client companies. I stayed home and worked on the book. He came back from time out in the world excited and gratified by his interactions with people. I had only my golden retriever Sunshine for stimulating company and spent the rest of my workdays alone with my typewriter, followed by the first Mac computer to hit the market. Tom would walk in the door and tell me about his daily adventures, then ask, "How was your day, dear?" I answered, "Well, I wrote four pages, ate a tuna fish sandwich, and walked the dog." There was something obviously wrong with this scenario. I hated it all, and never finished the book.

Then I started seeing a consultant who worked with high-achieving people who were dissatisfied with their career lives. That surely described me. After a month with Marta, from all our conversations I saw that I'm basically someone who is a producer who needs to work with other people and to be in charge. Sitting alone in a room for hours staring at a screen was no longer the gratifying path.

I narrowed my choices: Either I would start a shelter for abused women, or I would start a musical theatre company. I couldn't decide: one road seemed useful, the other frivolous. Marta asked this determining question: When I get up in the morning to go to work, which choice would make me happier?

So in 1995, I invented a theatre company called REPRISE, BROADWAY'S BEST. I had absolutely no idea what I was doing. I had an early love for and knowledge about musical theatre from growing up in New York. But I didn't know about stage left from stage right, and the only reason the project moved forward at all is that I was too dumb to be scared. I found some LA theatre folks who knew stuff, one pointed me towards the next one and everybody I met wanted to get involved. The basic idea flourished: We would do pared-down versions of classic, rarely revived musicals, with a one-week rehearsal period and one week of performances. We would lure stars who would be attracted to the short runs which wouldn't interfere with their tv or film lives.

I was blessed to find the right people: Somebody helped me set up a non-profit organization, somebody else found us the glorious Freud Theatre at UCLA. I took the renowned musical director Peter Matz to lunch to ask his advice about finding a musical director; he said, "Aren't you going to ask ME?" This man who had worked with Carol Burnett and Barbra

Streisand for years wanted to join our little troupe. I was amazed but soon realized REPRISE covered ground that was missing in LA theatre, and it was attracting solid professionals.

Peter opened a door for me to Jason Alexander of *Seinfeld* fame. Jason had a musical theatre history; he'd starred on Broadway in the Sondheim/Hal Prince musical *Merrily We Roll Along*. He had won a Tony for *Jerome Robbins' Broadway* and was aching to get back into the life. We had lunch. I asked him what shows he would like to star in, and he immediately suggested *Promises, Promises*, written by Hal David (his only musical) and Burt Bacharach.

I was later told by a cast member that he assumed I was a rich dilettante Beverly Hills hausfrau and I would fund the whole enterprise. That was probably because I really knew so little about what I was doing and was flying gutsy but blind. I remember sitting at meetings with the tech director, the lighting director, and the set designer and not having the slightest understanding of what was being discussed in depth. I faked it, took notes, and stayed silent. By the second show, I understood the world I was surrounded by and adored every minute of it.

We put together our first season: I wanted the second show to be *Finian's Rainbow*, because I'd performed in it in summer camp as a kid and loved the score. In fact, I could still sing every song. Our final show in the three-show season was *Wonderful Town*, another old gem I remembered from my childhood. REPRISE was a hit from the beginning, subscription sales were booming. The reviews were all that I could have wished for, and we were already discussing having a two-week run rather than one week, which we then inaugurated for the second season. A lot of stars wanted to work with us; Jean Smart and Fred Willard along with Jason Alexander in *Promises, Promises*; Andrea Marcovicci in *Finian's Rainbow*, Lucie Arnaz in *Wonderful Town*. I was in love with life, always thought how much more fabulous fun producing theatre was than sitting alone and writing all day.

Celebrity

I've wondered for years why everybody is so enchanted with celebrities. I include myself in that vast number. One could say, quite within reason, that a celebrity is merely someone who has acquired a football trophy, an agent, a hot mate, a multimillion deal in some category, or may be instead a person of real talent ranging from tiny to gigantic who captivates audiences.

You could also claim that we Americans are obsessed with someone's fame, whatever category they fall into. A bona fide movie star, certainly; a rock star perhaps even more so depending on your age. For example, I have no idea who the Foo Fighters rock group is, but I can go pretty goofy over Brad Pitt. Anything Kardashian leaves me cold.

The reasons for the common neurosis (sometimes psychosis) of celebrity lust are obvious: We think we're less fascinating than they, our lives more plebian, our experiences more drab. We assume they are happier than we are. Stepping into their shoes for a moment by reading *People* magazine may alter our sense of inferiority, but only temporarily. If we get to know a star, their loftiness or fame rubs off on us a bit.

Or conversely, maybe we feel more worldly and significant than we really are, and interacting with a celeb confirms that.

It might begin early in life, as a teenager when the basketball captain suddenly hugs you hard behind the chem lab and you are catapulted into a beauty you never felt before. You don't experience it as an assault, an insult, but rather a compliment. After all, he's the basketball superstar. And when you tell your girlfriends, they look at you with a new respect and perhaps awe. You are no longer the klutzy kid with a nose that's too wide. You are reborn into a special and desirable fifteen-year-old. That might be when your celebrity addiction is born.

You need more and more as you grow up, your smallish ego needs to be fed on a regular basis. You look for any connection with the famous stars you adore. You lust for connection with power folks and heroes.

If you go to a Broadway theatre, notice that after the performance dozens of autograph geeks gather at the stage door, sometimes waiting an hour, for the chance of a moment with the actors who are leaving the premises after the show. You might say that collecting a mere signature will remind the crowd of the pleasant experience they've just had. But the weird truth is that frequently the crowd hasn't even been inside the theatre for the show; they've just come for the autograph.

Once I was writing a piece for the *Washington Post* on Woody Allen, who was starring on Broadway in his play, *Play It Again, Sam*. The plan was that I would see the show, meet Woody backstage, and cross the street to Sardi's for the interview and late dinner. When we opened the stage door, he freaked out. At least fifty autograph crazies were waiting for him. He grabbed my arm, burrowed his little body next to mine, and pulled me fast across the street, while the crowd followed, at one point surrounding us, making it difficult to move forward. When we got to Sardi's, we bolted inside and the bouncers dispersed the crowd. We were both upset, of course, and downed a few strong drinks. "Does this happen after every performance?" I asked him as we both calmed down. "Yes," he answered in a throaty whisper. "Usually, I stay in my dressing room, sometimes for an hour, until they all leave."

I once met Richard Nixon, whose politics and sweaty upper lip I loathed. I was writing a cover story for the exalted *Life Magazine* about his daughter Tricia's wedding to some average guy whose name

I can't recall. Tricky Dick as he was nicknamed was President at the time. The White House that day—yes, it is the most glamorous and overwhelming building in America—was filled with all the notables that you can imagine while reading this. I won't name names but if you can remember that year, 1971, you will have heard of at least 300 of them.

The press was huddled behind barriers so that we could do our work but not mingle with the luminaries. Photography was forbidden. Yet we could see them and they us, and occasionally some publicity-starved, somewhat renowned guest would wave to us. I pretended to be too jaded to care when the vice-president, Spiro Agnew, shook my hand as I was on my way to the ladies' room.

I would love to meet President Biden, Adam Schiff, Nancy Pelosi, Senator Schumer, Elizabeth Warren at the Capitol. I might have to stifle myself from regaling each of them with what a remarkable job they're doing in these impossible times. But I certainly would not ask for their autographs. Or follow them across the halls of Congress. Would my sense of who I am expand or deepen if I had a conversation with Liz Cheney?

I have never asked a celebrity for his or her autograph. I've never approached a star in the shoe department of Saks Fifth Avenue to tell her how much I cherish her work. I did have sex once with a movie star who was staying at the same hotel as I in Madrid...

Sex...?

It's probably stupid to admit this, but I don't exactly remember having sex with Anthony Newley. Well, I do, vaguely, but only the memory of sex that one has in her inexperienced youth after being drunk on several cloying cocktails in quick succession at a raunchy bar in a raunchy neighborhood in Madrid.

How on earth did that happen to me, a kind of naive college girl who had just finished summer school at the University of Edinburgh studying medieval English literature? It was my first trip abroad and I had been bursting with everything European. London, Scotland, Paris, the countryside. So there I was in Spain with Linda, my best girlfriend from high school, and her eccentric brother Eddie, who drove us there from Paris, stopping for a night in

Andorra, the tiny country in the Alps between France and Spain that has had the longest life expectancy in the world.

At our funky Madrid hotel also lived the company from an American "spaghetti western" being filmed outside of the city. It was called *The Bandit of Zhobe* and it starred the fading Victor Mature, some other hungry cast and crew members, and a young bushy-haired Anthony Newley.

Linda and I were wined and dined by the company, nothing fancy for this low-budget movie thriller, but we were pretty much the only young American girls around the hotel. Also, we were taken out into the countryside to watch shooting a few times, with what a reviewer later called Senor Newley's "wince-inducing comic mugging" and Victor Mature's "smirking." This film was unlikely to win an Oscar. But it was always electrifying to us.

Then we were invited by Victor Mature to the opening of the giant bullring in the city, where all of us were treated like stars by the Madrid mayor and the audience. We sat in special boxes and waved to the matadors as they confronted the bulls. It was my first and last bullfight.

That same night I had sex with Anthony Newley. And, perhaps sadly, that's everything I remember. Linda and I left the next day for home and resumed our normal college existences. *The Bandit of Zhobe* didn't have much of a life.

Freud (Pronounced Frood) Playhouse

I am inside of the Freud Playhouse at UCLA at all hours, either watching rehearsals or performances of one of our frequent REPRISE musicals. Or I'm gabbing backstage with the company, actors who live for these moments but are tense, pacing, warming up for their songs, and hugging each other for support. The theatre has about 600 seats, medium-sized, but cozy. The seats are wide, with a great deal of space in front of each one so that the audience can spread out their legs. They are comfortable.

There are entrances from the front of the theatre for the audience and from the back for actors, crew, and production team. The lobby at the front is small—posters, snacks, and drinks are sold outside in the courtyard—and just contains a rack with the photos of the whole cast.

The Freud Playhouse is a magical place, like many theatres, whether filled or empty. You begin to be transported to the world on the stage before you find your seat. You feel unique anticipation and excitement when you enter, sit down, read the program, and wait for the show to begin. It is an experience unlike any other. But I especially like the Freud when it is empty, silent, and dark.

During the weeks of rehearsals, I'm usually sitting in the back of the dark theatre, taking notes, thinking, either happy or anxious—or both. I'm the producer, and I'm usually alone in the large space, not wanting to be distracted by anybody's comments, questions, or requests of me. The stage is buzzing with life, the tech folks setting up their lights, sound equipment, and simple scenery. I need to pay focused attention to everything.

During the rehearsal, the music always overwhelms me, whether played only on a piano or, near to opening night, with the orchestra. Sometimes I don't like a particular song or an actor's performance, and my head veers off into worrying about a million current issues, getting hazy with nerves. I'm tense about everything that could possibly go wrong or is actually going wrong. Why is Mary not singing her vowels clearly? Why does John forget his lyrics every time in that one song? My notes are unreadable scribbles. Fear races through my belly; then perhaps total bliss. Feelings travel back and forth like a spaceship during the course of one day.

Once the show opens, if it's going well, life becomes routine, I just show up at the theatre an hour before it starts, schmooze with the cast and the audience, be the comforting mom. Sometimes I don't stay until the end of the show, I don't need to see all two weeks of performances. Occasionally there's a huge problem, like the time the lead actress got an ominous, threatening note delivered to her backstage thirty minutes before the show. As we had no understudy, we had to cancel the performance and send everybody home, to reschedule for a later date.

Sometimes during the run of the show, I'm backstage waiting to go on to do my producer's curtain speech. My forehead is sweating, feet tapping intently. After all, I'm not an actor, I don't have those skills, and feel the weight of the planet on my shoulders. Am I talking too much? Being pretentious or even worse BORING? Is it cool asking for money for our non-profit company? Once, I forgot the name of the show's lyricist, my reeling mind just going blank. Thank God he wasn't in the audience that night.

One night, while waiting for the final seconds to walk onstage, the director whispered to me, "I'm giving you $50,000 so you can have a bigger orchestra." I was so astonished I could hardly focus on what I was saying. Another time a cast member who had been big trouble since the beginning was standing behind me and snickered in a stage whisper (which means loud enough for me to hear), "Why does she have to do this every night?" Again, I was disoriented but I had done my spiel so many times by then that I could usually run through it on semi-automatic. I confronted her after the show, and she apologized. I could tell she didn't mean it. I never worked with her again.

After my curtain speech and as the overture begins, I trot through the theatre to get to my second-row seat and ask Tom if I did all right, didn't screw anything up. He always grabs my hand and assures me I was perfect. Sometimes I believe him. The overture continues. Then, for two hours, I focus on the audience's reactions to everything. Are they clapping enough? Laughing robustly? Getting the jokes, cheering the songs? I keep glancing at the guy sitting to my left to gauge his reactions. If he's just blah or clearly bored I want to leave or maybe punch him. If he's jolly or teary or obviously having fun, I love him, and I'll keep sneaking looks at him to see if he got that joke or relished that song. I continue to look around the audience to connect with all the comforting familiar faces. I am home.

Sweeney Todd, The Demon Barber & Friends

In the spring of 1999 my theatre company, REPRISE, BROADWAY'S BEST, was given an awe-inspiring gig. I was asked, a year earlier by a director colleague who had a relationship with Stephen Sondheim, to produce five performances of *Sweeney Todd*, to celebrate its twentieth anniversary. Sondheim would come out from New York for the celebration and the grand Ahmanson Theatre at the LA Music Center would run the show.

I was bowled over, ecstatic and terrified, depending on the moment and what dark or light thoughts were jogging through my mind. I had never done anything this large, I knew we would be reaching out to create a cast of musical theatre stars, and—most nerve-wracking of all—would have to raise serious money to produce the show.

Sweeney Todd, The Demon Barber of Fleet Street, is my favorite musical, the *King Lear* of musical theatre. It won eight Tony Awards the season it opened on Broadway. I love the deep darkness, the insanity, the revenge moments, the remarkable humor, and every song.

We already had our *Sweeney* cast when I got involved. The deal had come with one of the biggest stars in television—Kelsey Grammer. Of course, nobody thought of him as a singer. In fact, since then, he has starred in several musicals, on Broadway (where he was nominated for a Tony for his role in *La Cage Aux Folles*) and off-Broadway. It was tantalizing for potential donors and ticket buyers to think of "Frasier" singing Sondheim's complex and bleak creation, and our marketing folks were delighted. Working with Kelsey was another story.

Christine Baranski signed on to play Mrs. Lovett and was a joy for the entire year preceding the production. She lived on the east coast but traveled to LA at least once a month to study the role with her favorite vocal teacher. When she finally arrived a few days before rehearsals began, she was probably ready to go onstage. With her combination of focused seriousness, dry wit, and upturned nose, she enchanted the whole company.

Rehearsals began: Kelsey had secured for us a sound stage at Paramount, the one where he filmed *Frasier*, which was now on hiatus. We would be working here for five days until we moved into the Ahmanson for onstage rehearsals with the orchestra, lights, sound, a simple set, and all the fixings for the production.

Did I mention that we only had ten days of rehearsal, a scant and scary schedule for such a daunting show? Kay Cole, our choreographer, and Calvin Remsberg, our director, created a blueprint three months before rehearsals began, which mapped out every move for every actor. Then, on the first day, we had to announce to the cast and the rest of the company that Kelsey would not be present for the next three days. He was building a home in Hawaii and was over there supervising that project. It was devastating, infuriating, and frightening to everybody.

My job, in normal circumstances, as producer, was to calmly oversee the rehearsals, to quietly make sure everything was working, that the intense activities each day proceeded smoothly. In the case of this production, my primary task was to prevent Christine from quitting, leaving the set, and flying back to her east coast home. I spoke with her agent every day, as did Larry Blank, our musical director, assuring him that it would all work out, Kelsey would return, he would know his role flawlessly, and Sweeney and Mrs. Lovett would put on a dazzling show for every thrilled theatregoer in Los Angeles.

Larry placated Christine by taking her out daily on the lunch breaks, sharing a martini, then having more martinis after rehearsal each day. We hired an actor to take Kelsey's place for the three days of his absence. Finally, he returned, after I had warned a few of the actors who were the most vocally pissed off at him, that for the sake of the show going on they should contain themselves and be nice. The immediate problem was that Kelsey didn't know his lines, his songs, or just about anything. We had, what the associate musical director Jerry Sternbach called "the most overqualified chorus in LA theatre history," with actors that normally played lead roles. Kelsey entered the room chewing gum and sang out of tune.

Days later the committed cast was splendid except for Kelsey. The amazing Melissa Manchester was playing the beggar woman, a significant role, Neil Patrick Harris was to be Tobias, Ken Howard played the villainous judge, the beautiful tenor Davis Gaines played Anthony the sailor. Every actor/singer in the cast was superior. Well, except for the lead. I had never experienced such an ill-prepared actor. Sleep did not come easily to me for two weeks.

There is a classic line of Sweeney's where, upon holding up his killer razor to the sky, he rails, "At last my arm is complete again." On a long chorus break one day, our stage manager gave the actors pads to draw on, and one actor took out his revenge on Kelsey by drawing a caricature of him raising his grand razor with the words, "AT LAST MY ARM IS... LINE PLEASE." The drawing made the rounds of the whole company, except for Kelsey. I wish I'd kept it.

Kelsey had a reputation, according to one of the directors of *Frasier*, for never knowing his lines, and frustrating the company. In the case of Kelsey as Sweeney Todd, we realized we would have to use what's called scrolling prompters each week, machines that live downstage between the performers and the audience. The prompter has the whole script and song lyrics, for the sake of the actor who, yes Kelsey, needs it for seeing his lines. We informed Kelsey he would have to pay for the prompters; he happily agreed.

It was amazing that Kelsey knew he was going to play Sweeney Todd a year before it happened. He "learned" it by singing along to a CD while riding in his limo between his Malibu home and Paramount Studios in Hollywood for his *Frasier* work.

A few days after we moved into the Ahmanson Theatre for rehearsals, Stephen Sondheim arrived. He came from New York for opening night, at which he would be getting an award from ASCAP. He watched a rehearsal from the back of the theatre. I sat next to him, agitated about how it would go since the day before we'd had to hire a kid to sit outside Kelsey's dressing room to warn him that he would be making his entrance in the next few moments. Sondheim didn't say a word to me during the entire run-through. Afterward, the cast came down into the theatre to greet him and he focused his attention on Kelsey, snarling, "Well, Kelsey, I guess you haven't sung much in the last twenty years." The rest of the company didn't hide their smirks.

The opening was to be a huge celebration for the twentieth anniversary, with a glamorous after-party, and several of us appearing on stage after the show's end to acknowledge Sondheim, including Angela Lansbury, the original Mrs. Lovett on Broadway, who had been hiding in the audience—we were worried Christine would be nervous if she knew Angela was there.

The run was completely sold out, the audience loved it, Christine was brilliant, Kelsey somehow sneaked through it and I didn't relax until the closing night cast party at a funky downtown Chinese restaurant, which we had asked Kelsey to pay for. He appeared for about fifteen minutes, then left.

Six months later I had a lunch date with Larry Blank, our superb musical director. As we greeted each other at the restaurant table, his first words to me were, "Stephen Sondheim never thanked me, he never thanked you, he only acknowledged the damn stage manager."

Hair:
Let The Sunshine In

During the year 2000, I made three trips to New York to secure the rights to produce *Hair* in Los Angeles. I went with Arthur Allan Seidelman, a highly-respected tv/film/theatre director who would be directing the REPRISE production, should the creators decide to give us the rights. I never understood the problem of getting these theatrical rights, we'd never had it with any other shows. REPRISE was a solid enterprise and *Hair* was still produced frequently since its inception in 1967. It might have been the fact that co-writer James Rado and composer Galt MacDermot didn't speak to each other, so a complexity was added to the negotiations that made extra trips and additional meetings necessary. It might be the inexplicable fact that Rado had been working non-stop on rewrites since the show's beginning more than thirty years previously. But finally, everybody agreed that we could produce the show and we moved joyfully ahead.

Hair, The American Tribal Love-Rock Musical was an enormous hit on Broadway in 1968, a game-changer, a new concept in musicals. It was the theatrical statement of the hippie counterculture of the 1960s, the anti-Vietnam war movement, the hallucinogenic drug scene, and the sexual revolution. Its "Aquarius" and "Let the Sunshine In" became the anthems of the rebellious times. The characters in the show were referred to as "the tribe" and were played as such, with bonding between everybody in the company, insisted upon by the director, the musical director Peter Matz and myself. Our *Hair* was going to be a celebratory love-in, nothing less.

We planned the production for the summer of 2001, six performances at the Wadsworth Theatre, a 1700-seat site on the grounds of the Veteran's Administration in West LA. It will be important to remember that the VA is controlled by the federal government. More later about that.

From the beginning, I had never been so excited planning a production. Auditions were sublime, the actors seemed more thrilled than their usual state of tension. On the second day as we went through the early round of actors on their callbacks, the associate musical director made everybody stand around the piano and improvise while we all watched carefully to see their spirit as well as their voices and how they blended with each other. This was really going to be a tribe, a team, a family.

The dramatic moment of the auditions came when I told the actors that they would all have to be nude for the finale of Act One. Everybody either smiled nervously or grinned happily except for Stephanie J. Block, currently a Broadway musical star, but at that time a competent local actor and singer. She was religious, we learned; she informed us she would not be taking her clothes off onstage, and she left the audition. I think the actors were relieved, one less competitor for a show that every singer, dancer, and actor under thirty-five in LA was aching to perform.

Arthur, the director, informed me he was going to bring in a young actor from New York, Eric Potter, specifically because of his experience with nude work in gay shows, his comfort level, and his well-endowed penis. In fact, a guy I knew came to opening night, and having seen this young stud, bought front row tickets for every subsequent performance.

Because the nude scene was being done in a federal building, we had to get permission from the government. They informed us that we could do a thirty-second bit, but no more. So, we never had the actors rehearse nude—their inauguration would be opening night.

The rehearsal period was like a scene from the

'60s Greenwich Village, flamboyant, somewhat wild, and of course grueling work. Everybody in the cast had grown their hair long and bushy and wigs were unnecessary. Jim Rado, the co-lyricist and co-book writer, was onsite the entire time, annoying everyone and intruding on the process. One afternoon, when we were all high from a particularly gorgeous scene with a heart-stirring song, he tried to soul kiss me; it was the last time I got anywhere near his face.

He jumped on the stage whenever he had a comment for the cast, ignoring the director. I had to take him aside and assure him he was a valuable guest but was not directing this production. He continued with his interference at those moments when he was overcome with his creation, his power. Jim and his partner, Galt MacDermot, were never onsite at the same time; they were indeed enemies. Galt came to the opening with the original choreographer, who was pissed off she hadn't been hired for this production.

Hair sold out as soon as it was advertised. Some of our actors were discovered for Broadway because of the show; Steven Weber replaced Matthew Broderick in *The Producers*, Marissa Jaret Winokur got a leading role in *Hairspray*. People brought their young kids to a performance—I was alarmed when I saw a ten-year-old with his dad, a scruffy, long-haired throwback to the '60s, both in tie-dyed t-shirts and torn jeans. And a middle-aged couple on a motorcycle, their faces painted many colors, like rainbows. I was a '60s creature as well as they, but this recycling of the grand old days still flummoxed me.

One of the actors' parents, conservative Midwestern folks, came out from Iowa for the show. Their son was a handsome young man; I met them in the lobby pre-show, and I worried. "Well, they're just going to see it all, aren't they," Arthur our director tried to reassure me. At intermission, I hid from them.

Back to the nude scene, several reminiscences: At intermission, our Board of Directors' attorney, a very savvy movie biz guy, pulled me aside and grumped, "The nude scene was supposed to be thirty seconds according to the feds. I timed it; it was twelve minutes!" I tried to look upset and surprised, but all I was thinking was that by the time the news got back to the bureaucracy in Washington, if it ever did, the show's run would be over. But meanwhile, everybody was talking about it. Sam Harris, one of the leads told me, "I keep fucking up the lyrics to the song, I'm so distracted by being naked." I said, "Stop worrying, Sam, nobody's listening." One of the cast masturbated before he came out, so his penis would grow. I felt grateful that I didn't know about this event until after the run was finished.

Arthur had designed the show so that the audience and performers would be as one with little distance between them. The actors came onstage in the beginning by cavorting through the audience, stopping to say hello or give a fist bump while the overture played. After the finale, when the actors took bows, I ran up onstage from the audience and we all danced and hugged. Frequently, an overcome audience member would also jump on the stage and dance wildly. Nobody had seen anything like this before in a theatre. *Hair* was a unique experience. It was simply glorious, unforgettable. It altered my life as a producer forever, after knowing what remarkable joy this musical theatre world could be.

Roxie

Roxie, the Beloved

I know you think your dog is the most adorable pooch in the world. And that you love her/him more than anybody in the world loves her/his dog. I'm very sorry to say that you are wrong. My eighteen-pound mutt, Roxie, is not only the cutest, most special doggie on the planet, but also the most beloved.

She is seven years old, shiny black, with large brown eyes; her most distinguishing feature is her giant Papillon ears which stop people on the street to comment. A bit of background: I only had golden retrievers in my adult dog life: grand, gorgeous, sweet animals. When my last one, Mollie, passed at age sixteen after a bout with lymphoma, Tom and I decided to go smaller, given our advancing years. We always rescue dogs, as opposed to buying them, so I began the search right after Mollie died. I am someone who can't live without the presence of a dog for very long.

A week after we put out the word, when our home felt empty and dull, our lawyer's wife emailed me. She rescues and fosters dogs, looking for the best homes for them. She sent me photos of several small dogs, Roxie among them. She said she would bring a few to our home the next day, for us to meet. Tom was going to be away from home all day with work appointments, so he anointed me to choose a dog if one struck my fancy. Tom is not a dog nut case as I am, although he certainly loved all our goldens. But I'm someone who, at a party, will give a serious amount of attention to any dogs roaming around, in lieu of focusing on the guests. You who are dog nuts will know exactly what I'm talking about.

When Marilyn arrived with three dogs, all very dear, we stood outside our condo building and watched the trio frolic on the beach. Roxie sprinted to me and jumped up on me, staring into my eyes with her huge brown ones, and that was it, I was in love. Marilyn had brought food, a little bed, all the tools and toys that a new home would require. Tom came home a few hours later, took one glance at her, and has said many times since then, "Something in my heart I didn't even know was there opened up and I was flooded with love." He became a Roxie nut case. That was six years ago.

We frolicked endlessly with Roxie for two days,

scratching her belly whenever she rolled over on the bed or couch. I put a small bed next to my desk and she spent as much of the day there as I spent next to her. She was calm, easy, perfect.

Two days later Tom got a call from our attorney who, with much embarrassment, said: "Marilyn has been crying since she gave you Roxie. She misses her terribly and really wants her back. Can you possibly return her?" Tom ran into my office and told me of the call. I responded in a loud unpleasant voice, "NO F—ING WAY. What is she doing fostering dogs if she's getting so attached?" I ranted on about Marilyn, and her unfitness to be a mother, albeit a temporary one, until Tom called our attorney back and rejected his request, in more civil words than I had used. A few days later I got an email from Marilyn, offering to find me another dog. It was a civil letter, she acknowledged her inappropriateness—but still wanted Roxie back. I declined of course. We didn't communicate for a few more years until I bumped into her at a concert, showed her photos of Roxie, and had a lovely exchange. She was still fostering dogs.

Roxie is our beloved, probably the second most important being in my life. We walk by the shore with her while she chases birds and engages other doggies to play and yaps occasionally at folks who, I insist to Tom, are undoubtedly bad people; she sleeps sometimes on my head but always on the bed between us, sometimes working her way under the covers to curl up on my feet. She jumps on my chest in the morning when I wake up and she senses it might be time for a walk. Our friend Stef prepares her food, a natural human diet; she eats healthier than we do. She is almost always peaceful and, I think, content.

Once, a few years ago, while I walked her on the path in front of our home, she nipped a woman who was strange and was yelling continuously at nothing. A neighbor, Janet, who is the local troublemaker, saw this minor event and convinced the woman to report us to the police. We had to go to court, brought with us several statements from friends who knew Roxie well and loved her deeply. The case was dismissed; Janet and I haven't spoken to each other since. She has a dog named Goliath.

Twice a week, we send Roxie out with Alan, a master hiker who loads about eight dogs in his van and goes up into the Santa Monica mountains for six hours. Whatever they do and wherever they go, Roxie comes back exhausted, and collapses for hours on the bed.

Sometimes she and I lie side by side on the bed and look deeply into each other's eyes for several moments. Most dogs don't like to do that; it's threatening to them, I'm told. But Roxie of course isn't like most dogs. I'm dying to know what she's thinking, what she's feeling about me and about her life. Does she love me more than I love her? Is that even possible? Is she happy? Isn't it a wonderful thing that I never wanted children?

Alan, the Dog Hiker

Alan is the happiest person I know. Six days a week he is doing exactly what he loves doing in life, all day long. I don't know what he does on the seventh, but I'm sure that he's not as delighted or blissful as he is Monday through Saturday.

What he does that makes him so ecstatic about his life is to is go hiking with dogs, our precious Roxie included.

I met him on the path in front of my home while I was walking Roxie, shortly after we rescued her six years ago. He was trotting with a golden retriever at his side and when we chatted, he told me he took dogs into the mountains and hills above Malibu every day, all day. I had already noticed that Roxie loved running, and although only eighteen pounds, she outran every dog on the beach by our home and required that much exercise. So, I was sold on Alan. I could also tell that his love for his "clients" was profound. Since then, Alan has picked Roxie up every Tuesday and Friday morning at about 10:00 and returns her a bit before dark.

I don't know precisely where they go, or what they do when they get there. I do know that on her return home she falls asleep on our bed immediately, and sometimes doesn't even get up for dinner. I also know that if you make the earnest mistake of asking, "Where are you walking the dogs today?" or "Did you all have a good walk?" he will become peeved and won't try to conceal it. He will say, with a grimace, "I'm not a dog walker, I'm a dog hiker." The distinction is meaningful to him and was difficult for me to understand until I joined him and learned the difference between a mere walk and a very serious hike.

Once, only once, I went along with Alan and eight dogs, all piled up in the back of his aromatic van. Sometimes he takes as many as ten. They were mostly big animals, German shepherds, huskies, one named Rambo who is a wolf—not a wolf-dog which is somewhat common around the beach—but a full-fledged wolf. They were all amiable, joyous, and little Roxie fit in just fine. He drove us up into a canyon just off the Pacific Coast Highway near Malibu, he changed from his sandals to serious workout shoes, and after we hit the trail he removed the short leashes from the dogs and let them run free. I struggled to keep up with everybody. The dogs were in his peaceful control; nobody scampered away, lagged behind, or fought with the others. They were a true pack. Roxie was in heaven. Alan, who is in great shape, jogged along with them. Me, not so much. I could tell he doesn't really like to hike with people; in fact, I'm told he never encourages it when anybody seems interested. After this one time, I never wanted to go with Alan and the pups again.

At one point, when we came to a lovely vista, he did something I found improbable to believe: He took out his cell phone, instructed the dogs to all line up on the rocks facing him, and to stay perfectly still while he took several photos. It looked like a graduation class or a chorus line. Nobody broke away and bolted, played with the other dogs, or disobeyed his calm voice. Every dog faced Alan and the camera and didn't move. He does this on every hike. He even lines them up in size order, so Roxie is always in the front row, Rambo the wolf in the rear.

When I joined him on that one adventure, as we drove to the hiking trail up the highway and into the mountains, Alan told me his life story. He had worked once in the aerospace industry as an executive at Northrop in Los Angeles. He was marching up the corporate ladder when, as a young man in his thirties he developed cancer and while being treated, he decided to become fit and do something he was passionate about. Dogs were the only answer for him and still are. His decision made great sense to me. He has found where he belongs.

I have said he's the happiest man I know. I know that Roxie yaps with adoration when he comes to pick her up, he hugs her and kisses her head when he returns her. I always have the sense when I watch this interaction, that there's a sadness in him at having to say goodbye to her. But, of course, he'll be greeting another adored pack the next morning and the morning after that. Soon, he'll be greeting our Roxie once again and having a magical day with his gang.

Reflections

On Gratitude

The cheerful watchword of the past two years has been "gratitude." With all our complaints, anxieties, loneliness, depression, overeating, and compulsive Netflix watching, we are told by experts to be consciously and frequently grateful for what we have, not as some silly bromide but as a means to increase our health and mental/emotional stability. I even saw a recent tv ad for mattresses that spoke of gratitude.

The online articles have been profuse. One says that "grateful people take better care of themselves and engage in more protective health behaviors like regular exercise, a healthy diet, regular physical examinations." Another spoke of the virtue of keeping a weekly gratitude journal. (I'm grateful I don't feel compelled to do this every single day, my cynical brain reports). Another, which makes sense to me, talks of creating a list of all the benefits in our lives and asking ourselves to what extent do we take these for granted?

A UC Davis psychology professor says that the practice of gratitude can lower blood pressure, improve immunity, and help the quality of one's sleep. He also says that "people who keep a gratitude journal have a reduced dietary fat intake...Stress hormones like cortisol are twenty-three percent lower in grateful people. And having a daily gratitude practice could actually reduce the effects of aging to the brain." Grateful people, he claims, are generally more optimistic. Optimism, they say, creates more disease-fighting cells in our bodies.

I agree, I think. The experts, masters of "positive psychology", tell us to think of one thing or person we're grateful for when we wake up and before we go to sleep. And take a few moments every day to meditate on grateful thoughts. Move our minds from thinking about gratitude occasionally to making it part of our frequent or second nature. A doctor and author of *The Mayo Clinic Handbook for Happiness*, talks about "sprinkling a little gratitude throughout your day," as a way of decreasing one's risk of disease.

Tom and I do a daily affirmation in bed each morning that we're at home together. We've been doing this for forty years. The only time we don't is if one of us is getting up extremely early or is out of town. We call it our "Aff" for short, and it's a crucial ritual in our lives. First, we each affirm our intention for the day (to be creative, calm, productive, kind, stress-free—all good stuff). Then we say everything we're grateful for: each other, our good albeit aging health, Roxie our dog, friends and family, our work, the people who help us keep our lives together, our home on the beach. And more. Then we ask, "what can I do to make you happy today?" When we began adding that question to the Aff, we answered with items like "You can take your shirts to the laundry," or "You can pick up some cheddar cheese at the market." Then we realized how pedestrian and self-centered that sounded so we shifted to noble thoughts like "you can enjoy everything you do, you can take some time to exercise, you can realize how much I think about you." That works a lot better than the laundry request.

One of the gratitude mavens advises making a "gratitude jar", which keeps an empty jar and paper in an accessible place at home, asking those we live with to write a single thing they're grateful for every day and putting it in the jar. Every day we should read the contents of the jar aloud. And try to be funny. I'm sure that I will never do this, but I don't know why. The same authority recommends creating reminders, like nearby photos of people to whom we're connected, or inspirational quotes, and keeping them on the fridge or by one's computer. I like the idea of photos, not so much the quotes. And I hate stuff that's loitering on the fridge door.

I think that by nature I'm not an inherently grateful person. To begin with, I am Jewish as you know, and thus have an abiding and ancient level of trepidation, no matter the situation. That is compounded by the history of my Russian immigrant family, one of turmoil, not ease. But my current circumstances are pretty great most of the time. Without detailing the benefits of my life, which would risk my being despised by most readers, let's just say I have an excellent life. But feeling gratitude as my second nature is not my lifelong way of being. I tend to experience the vulnerability of anxiety, manifesting itself as a nervous belly. The occurrence can be anything from what happened the other day when I discovered the left front bumper of my car was coming apart from no apparent cause, or a recurrent fear that our dog is going to run into the street—which she has never done in six years and doesn't walk by the street anyway. Or a constant terror of what's happening to our country. Would a practice of gratitude lessen these stressors? I have no idea.

To be grateful for one's blessings on a daily basis would probably be to know balance and perspective. To lighten up, to appreciate, to understand excellent luck as well as forbearance. To really experience one's good fortune. To make the connection between fine health and the virtues of gratitude. To appreciate Tom and all his lovely qualities, as well as our daily affirmation. I may not put notes in a gratitude jar, but I can surely manage to understand how to create lower blood pressure, less daily fat intake, and a boosted immune system. For all that I'm very grateful.

Extroversion

I was a shy child. I rarely raised my hand in class, I sat in the back of the room whenever I could. In groups of kids, I hung back, pretended to be part of the gang, but was scared and spoke little. I thought I was less pretty than all the other girls, and so assumed I was less appealing to the boys. This world lasted until high school, when by some miracle I came out of my withdrawn shell, and became part of activities, playing the piano at concerts in the school auditorium, accompanying kids who were singing or dancing. I got big attention for this and craved it more and more. I was no longer desperately shy. I've never understood why this overnight transformation occurred, but I was certainly relieved that it did. My personality changed.

A few years ago, I took something called The Harrison Preference Profile which, among other assessments, measures one's personality type. I was surprised to learn that I'm categorized in this report as an extreme extrovert, an assessment that was surely belied by my childhood.

Like almost everybody else on the planet during the pandemic lockdown and until we had all our vaccinations, Tom and I stayed home. We worked in our separate offices, didn't let anybody new enter our condo, ordered our food and supplies via Instacart, watched Hulu and Amazon Prime almost every night. We had two couple friends in our tiny bubble whom we saw once a week each, usually, like in the case of our neighbors Susan and Steve, outside on the beach for wine and snacks. Friendships and family gatherings were all on Zoom. And like almost everybody that I knew, I was miserable. I lapsed into a depressed introversion. The feedback about my extroverted instincts I had gotten from the Harrison Profile was the distinct opposite of the woman I became after March 2020.

Yes, I missed movies, museums, theatre, and concerts. But what was most painful was not seeing friends, going to parties and restaurants, giving dinners for eight. Above all else, I missed our singing parties.

For years pre-Covid, we created these events every four months or so. Our friend Jerry, a marvelous pianist, was the central figure as he accompanied all the singing. Professional friends did solo performances, usually Broadway musical songs, while the rest of us joined in from the outskirts surrounding the piano. If I'd had enough wine, I would perform a solo number from a Stephen Sondheim show, which I often regretted later as I wasn't all that brilliant. We felt blessed to have this world of musical pals. (Recently, two friends who are professional singers told me they felt pressure at our parties to perform and only wanted to be part of the audience gang. Ah, well...)

We gave our first singing party in more than a year just a few weeks before the Omicron variant appeared. A glorious event, twenty-five vaccinated buddies hugged, sang, reveled in feeling free and being together. It was bliss for Tom and me. I even sang a solo of "Adelaide's Lament" from *Guys and Dolls*. I'd had several glasses of chardonnay beforehand.

In my life as a theatrical producer, I would often be onstage. Not as an actor, God forbid, but giving the curtain speech introducing the show. I'm always jittery before walking onstage, as I know many true actors are, trickles of sweat sitting on my temples. But the extrovert in me is calm as soon as I'm out there, in tune with the audience faces that I can only see in the shadow of the bright lights, but which always feel welcoming.

I recently heard that Cher is so terrified before she goes onstage for her concerts, that she has an assistant who literally pushes her out, at which point she transforms into Cher, the glittering star.

Tom grew up as a neighbor in Beverly Hills to the genius actor/performer Danny Kaye. Tom was best friends with his daughter Dena and was sometimes invited to their lavish parties populated with TV and movie stars. Tom said that Kaye spent most of the party sitting in his kitchen with his daughter and Tom, not in the living room with his guests, and leaving the hosting social duties to his wife, Sylvia.

Tom has been categorized, by the Harrison Assessment, as an introvert. I was surprised by this outcome, but he felt it was accurate. As a business consultant, he works with people most of the day, these months on Zoom. But he says, "I've trained myself to be extroverted, for work, but I'd always rather sit in the corner at a gathering, just talking to one person. I don't feel comfortable being in a sizable crowd."

I wonder if anybody really does feel at home and outgoing in that situation.

I can think of one circumstance where I become introverted. When I'm with a small group where one person is dominating the conversation to the exclusion of everyone else, I withdraw and mentally exit the room—unless his or her speechifying is fascinating, in which case I abandon any notion of interacting, and surrender to just being a good listener. But this rarely happens. People who consume the conversation at a dinner party, for example, are rarely that interesting.

My good friend Jon, who is a clergyman, writer,

teacher, and comedy performer says, on this subject, "I'm an overcompensating introvert. I'm really comfortable in front of an audience, where I feel in control." And he's happy in one-on-one conversations. Middle size groups, of about ten people, where he's not the star, are harder for him. "I've learned to be charming, but being social is a constant choice, an effort, it's not natural for me."

I'm reminded of all the tales of former President Bill Clinton that I've heard from several folks who have been around him. He seems to be the consummate extrovert. Even in a large crowd, he can focus all his attention on one person such that she or he feels that they are the only one in the room and that Bill finds them amazing. This has always been described as one of his looming gifts.

In a crowd I will always look for people I know and create a conversation with them. If there isn't anybody, I'll look for a woman who appears welcoming and accessible, whose outfit I like. Particularly her shoes. I think even a committed extrovert has her standards.

So in this crazy time we're living in, I swing between introversion and my natural extroversion, between wearing green eye shadow and cool outfits when we go out to dinner with friends, and just wearing sweatpants and a blank face. There's frequently a moment before it's time to leave home when I'm relaxing on my bed and I think, "Oh, why can't we stay home and just watch our latest Netflix obsession?"

How about assuming we all have both aspects in us of introvert and extrovert, and one gets awakened at specific times and places. Let's do that and not fret over what category defines us. Meanwhile, I'm going out to dinner with some scintillating pals...

How to Be
A Jewish Woman

I am a frequently confused Jewish woman. I've always identified as Jewish, was raised Jewish and will continue to be so until the afterlife—whatever and whenever that is. My family, in my growing up years, belonged to the local synagogue in our small suburban town. We went to services only on the two High Holy Days, Rosh Hashana and Yom Kippur, (everybody pronounced Kippur "kipper" like the fish). In my cynical teenage years, I believed our attendance was rooted solely in my mother's commitment to wearing her mink stole.

When I left home for the University of Wisconsin, I abandoned any form of my past Judaism. Although my roommate Shelley was Canadian Jewish, most of my dates were midwestern fair-haired "goys" as I grew up labeling Gentile, non-Jewish folks. (There was no prejudice or scorn in the word "goy", it was merely an abbreviation for "goyish." Well, maybe there was SOME condescension in that label.)

Roommate Shelley and I embarked on a journey of resistance against all our growing-up values. We found several Buddhist gurus to chant with on our vast campus, I meditated, and I drank a ridiculous amount of beer, which I'd never even tasted in my earlier life but was plentiful in our Milwaukee environs. I think there was a synagogue near the campus, but it never had my presence in the two years I was there.

Nonetheless, I was Jewish in my bones. As much as I was and am female, white, and American, being Jewish is a solid, unwavering part of my identity. But I'm not observant, I don't understand my relationship to God, and it's only once a year that I experience a deep connection with my Judaism.

When I was twenty-one and just out of college I lived in Jerusalem for a year, worked for a local newspaper at the Eichmann trial, and dated a Sabra—a native Israeli. In the beginning I was shocked that Israeli Jewish had little to do with observant, religious Jewish for almost all its citizens. None of my new friends had a seder, went to synagogue, or commemorated the High Holy Days. They celebrated Israeli Independence Day and on Yom Kippur when offices were closed, we went to the beach. It made sense in that culture, I realized, but it was a step in my confusion. Who was I, I often questioned?

Cut to my life of the last forty years. I married a Jewish man, as I always knew in my heart that I would. He came from a Beverly Hills background: his parents belonged to the most exclusive Jewish country club in the city and attended the most prestigious synagogue in town. But Tom's family was like my family, Jewish but not exactly Jewish except a few times a year. Tom's path, as mine, was definitely one you could label "Jewish Light".

At one point in his twenties he was living with a Gentile woman and her two kids on the east coast and celebrated Christmas, along with a highly decorated tree. I found that startling. I had never celebrated Christmas. But then again, I'd never observed Hanukah, our equivalent, which goes on for eight days instead of one. I don't even really know what it is, this Festival of Lights. Am I really Jewish? Am I a bad Jew?

When we were first married, Tom asked that we have a Christmas tree for our annual holiday party. I was extremely uncomfortable and after two years I demanded that we not do this again. We never have.

I might judge myself as a terrible Jew except for my deep relationship to Passover. Passover, to simplify, commemorates the Jews' liberation from slavery in Egypt. It's a joyous holiday, the first night (or two nights, depending on your commitment) being the seder. I am the most passionate seder hostess in

LA, I'm quite sure. Indeed, one of the most painful Covid lockdown experiences of 2020 for me was having to do a Zoom seder in April with ten friends. It was quite depressing.

My love for the seder began, as all of this Jewish journey did, in my childhood. My Aunt Lillian and Uncle Harold, who lived in Manhattan, always held a seder. It was our one family ritual of the year. The responsive reading of the Haggadah, which is the text explaining the Passover story, was exciting to me. The relatives always complimented me, as the youngest, for my pronunciation of Hebrew words. The singing was boisterous. I adored every minute of it, as I cherish the seder that Tom and I host each year.

I spend several days preparing the foods that are part of the "seder plate", which is the basic ingredient of the ritual. We own a lovely large blue glass plate with separate sections for the bits of the food: a few sprigs of parsley (symbolizing gratitude for the fruit of the earth); charoset, a mixture of fruit, nuts and wine, expressing the sweetness of life; a roasted egg for fertility; sharp horseradish embodying the bitterness of slavery; and a cooked lamb bone denoting the sacrifices of the Jews. The primary food ingredient of the seder is the matzo, unleavened bread speaking to the Jews' inability during their escape from Egypt to find the time to bake bread. I only eat matzo during the seven days of Passover, when regular baked goods are forbidden. It's not a thrilling food.

I cook chicken soup, whose only real function is to contain the matzo balls, a favorite sublime Jewish creation. Tom and I always make the matzo balls together, which last year—in our first dinner party since Covid—tasted fine but looked like squashed golf balls. We laughed and thought about redoing them but assumed our pals would scarf them down without criticism. They did.

We always have eight friends at the seder. About half are usually not Jewish. The seder is led by Tom's best friend the aforementioned Jon, a Jewish Unitarian minister, scholar, and writer. He melds together the fundamental similarities of Judaism, Christianity, and Islam—did you know that the Last Supper was a seder?—and interprets the Haggadah book, which we all read aloud going around the table. I chant the classic Four Questions in Hebrew—"Why is this night different from all other nights?" It's my main solo performance of the evening. It's also the only Hebrew I know.

Every year I learn something new from our wise and scholarly buddy Jon, who, by the way, also brings the heavenly brisket. And all our friends clamor to be invited. It is the night of the year I feel the most connected to being a Jew, and not being at all confused. I know then who I am and who I always will be.

September 28, 2020
Yom Kippur

I want to believe in God. What serenity that might bring—I think. A sense of order or alrightness in this chaotic world, a belief in God would calm my anxious belly and mind. I think I wouldn't worry so much about the future of our crazy country. I want to believe that everything happens for a reason, even the darkest calamities, the unthinkable injustices, the tragedies. I want to believe there's another life beyond this one, where things are rosy, and even though I won't have a body I'll still be able to cavort with the friends and family I've lost and meet new terrific bodiless people.

But I always return to "What God would have permitted Auschwitz?" There is simply no answer to that eternal question and never will be. Today I ask "what God would have allowed or even created this horrific virus? What God would have permitted Donald Trump or Vladimir Putin? What God would be allowing human beings the soulless destruction of the earth? How do rabbis and scholars answer these questions today for themselves and the people who look to them? With my advancing age, I think about "what's next" all the time. I have no answer, nor does anybody, really. I don't care what all the shamans and gurus and holy people say, they're making it up like the rest of us.

On Yom Kippur, the most holy Jewish holiday, Tom, Roxie and I will walk by the shore to the Venice Pier at low tide as we do a few times a week. I am barefoot, splashing my feet in the glistening waves. My sweatpants are getting soaked up to my knees, but it feels great. Roxie gallops back and forth in the water, yapping at the birds. She is so fast for an 18-pound pup that people stop and gaze at her, laughing. A sad-looking man pulling an ice cream wagon is trudging across the soft sand. I've never seen anybody buy anything from him. Often, I feel as if I'm living for this walk, even though at night my right knee will need special concern. I don't care. Our beach walk lifts my spirit and comforts my soul. I need that.

God has always existed only in nature for me. Oceans, beaches, mountains, snow—beauty not created by humans. We look at the moon beaming on the water before we go to bed. I sometimes see God then. Only then.

A Letter to Marcia

Dear Marcia,

I've been feeling that I should be communicating with you more frequently. I, of course, am you, but the self of you that may be hidden, disguised, or just ignored. Not the self of you that you show to the outer world which sometimes is not your true or complete self.

So let's get started. For one thing, you are a high-functioning pessimist. This is more apparent to me over the past two years, when optimism was and is still hard to come by. President Biden in a press conference last year rolled up his sleeve and took his booster vaccine shot in front of the world. He also told the press that he's a natural optimist, he's sure that everything will work out well. Who knows if he means this, given the nightmare scenarios on his plate. But for now, let's take him at his word.

You, Marcia, of course, do not have the President's potentially catastrophic events in your life; in comparison, you have small, insignificant items to contend with: the $300 check you sent someone which never arrived and may have been stolen from your outgoing mailroom slot because those things have been happening lately; Tom's recent pattern of losing things, like his iPhone, which he dropped in his doctor's office and it vanished; Roxie's periodic nipping at your housekeeper's ankles; your chicken-bone cranky right knee. These are the sorts of items that keep you awake at night.

But there are also the old-age memory concerns that prevent a long, contented sleep: forgetting words, like the name of the egg dish you had for your brunch with friends yesterday at the Waldorf Hotel; the title of the show you want to see that's opening soon, or the book you're listening to on Audible, or the name of one of your neighbors whom you've known for fifteen years. The forgotten words usually come back to you after a few moments, or you ask Tom and he reminds you. Nonetheless, it's a pretty constant worry.

You're also very concerned about the looming nightmares in our country's life, like the reality of Donald Trump running again for President and OMIGOD winning. And of course, the end of *Roe v.*

Wade as more states make abortion illegal again and the right-wing Supreme Court makes it happen. And the unspeakable disaster in Ukraine. I know you can hardly think about that without tearing up.

I said earlier that you're a high-functioning pessimist. How do you explain how lucky, successful, and creative you've been in your life, and still you frequently focus on the dark side? I have no idea. Perhaps they're not related at all. Or maybe most very productive people, if they were to admit or confront it, have a pessimistic foundation that they work to overcome. As I said, I have no idea.

You've always galloped straight ahead into life, into worlds that were new and scary to you. Like creating a successful theatre company when you didn't know stage left from stage right. You just wanted to do it, to make this giant leap in your work, away from being a long-time journalist, and you were smart enough to surround yourself with people who knew much more about it than you. Were you terrified that it wouldn't flourish, did you lose months of calm sleep, eat too much pie, clutch onto Tom, feel desperate and alone? Probably, that would be consistent with who you are, but I don't really remember. I do remember the remarkable joy you always had producing theatre for years.

Marcia dear heart, I know you're struggling with getting older. You're officially OLD with all the obvious traumas that are carried with the title. We won't talk here about the Big One.

It's true your friends compliment you on your "life force" and your energy and sometimes you can experience that yourself. You still want to work, write, produce theatre. But something's changed. You don't have all that vital verve you used to, long walks have gotten shorter, body aches in dozens of places occur without warning. You sit at lunch with your funny girlfriends and your conversations always begin with "the organ recital" of pains and ailments. You all try to remember the title of that movie you saw starring what's-his-name.

You worry about loss, and you must force yourself not to continue speeding down that highway. You, Tom, Roxie, and all your great dear friends and little family are healthy enough for you not to be very concerned right now. Your blessings abound and gratitude is something you and Tom practice every morning. Silence the pessimist if you are able, cheer yourself up with a creamy pasta dinner and a fine HBO movie and I hope you sleep well tonight, Marcia. Remember, I'm always here for you.

Love,

Marcia

About the Author

Marcia Seligson has written nine books, including the best-seller *The Eternal Bliss Machine, America's Way of Wedding* and articles for virtually every major magazine and newspaper in America. A lifelong lover of musical theatre, she created REPRISE: BROADWAY'S BEST in Los Angeles and served as the Producing Artistic Director for over forty events. She has produced new works on and off-Broadway and co-founded the Festival of New American Musicals.

www.marciaseligson.com